YELLOWSTONE WILDLIFE
A Watcher's Guide

By Todd Wilkinson
Photography by Michael H. Francis

NORTHWORD
PRESS, INC
P.O. Box 1360, Minocqua, WI 54548

Library of Congress Cataloging-in-Publication Data

Wilkinson, Todd.
    Yellowstone wildlife :   a watcher's guide / by Todd Wilkinson ;
[photography by Michael H. Francis].
        p.   cm.
    Includes bibliographical references.
    ISBN 1-55971-140-X : $11.95
        1. Zoology--Yellowstone National Park.   2. Wildlife watching-
-Yellowstone National Park--Guidebooks.   I. Francis, Michael H.
(Michael Harlowe), 1953-   . II. Title.
QL215.W55   1992
599.09787'52--dc20   92-4010
                                                                  CIP

Edited by Greg Linder
Designed by Russell S. Kuepper

All photography by Michael H. Francis except
pp. 68, 70, 71, 72, 80, 86, and 90 (center and bottom)
provided by Robert W. Baldwin.

For a free catalog describing NorthWord's
line of nature books and gifts, call 1-800-336-5666

ISBN 1-55971-140-X

Printed and bound in Singapore

TABLE OF CONTENTS

YELLOWSTONE MAP 8
INTRODUCTION 10

MAMMALS
Grizzly Bear 22
Black Bear 27
Gray Wolf 30
Coyote 32
Red Fox 34
Mountain Lion 36
Bobcat 38
Lynx 40
Bison 42
Moose 45
Elk (Wapiti) 48
Pronghorn (Antelope) 52
Mule Deer 55
White-tailed Deer 58
Bighorn Sheep 59
Mountain Goat 62

BIRDS
Bald Eagle 64
Golden Eagle 68
Osprey 70
Red-tailed Hawk 71
Peregrine Falcon 72
Great Gray Owl 74
American White Pelican 76
Great Blue Heron 78
Sandhill Crane 80
Trumpeter Swan 82
Canada Goose 86

A YELLOWSTONE GALLERY 88

SO YOU'D LIKE TO KNOW MORE? 94

BIBLIOGRAPHY 95

About the Author and Photographer

Author **Todd Wilkinson** came to Yellowstone to work as a summer park concession employee while he was attending St. Olaf College in Northfield, Minnesota. Today, he lives in Bozeman, Montana, located 90 miles north of the national park, and writes regularly about wildlife and natural history for a number of national magazines and newspapers. He is the northern Rockies correspondent for *The Denver Post* and a contributing editor to *Backpacker* magazine. *Yellowstone Wildlife* is his second book. His first, titled *Greater Yellowstone National Forests*, was published in 1991.

Photographer **Michael H. Francis** was born in Maine, but he has spent the past quarter of a century as a resident of Montana. Mike is a graduate of Montana State University, and worked seasonally in Yellowstone National Park for 15 years before becoming a fulltime wildlife photographer. His fine photography has been published by the National Geographic Society, the Nature Conservancy, the Audubon Society, the National Wildlife Federation, and NorthWord Press, among many others. He was the sole photographer for *Elk Country* and *Mule Deer Country*, natural history titles previously published by NorthWord.

Acknowledgments

In particular, the author extends warm thanks to Yellowstone research specialist Norm Bishop, park ornithologist Terry McEneaney, and Yellowstone's former assistant chief ranger Gary Brown for graciously reviewing the manuscript and offering valuable suggestions. Appreciation also is directed toward the National Park Service, U.S. Fish and Wildlife Service, and U.S. Forest Service for the information those agencies supplied. As always, Yellowstone's chief spokesperson Joan Anzelmo and her staff have provided crucial access to park officials and information. Thanks, too, are in order to Yellowtone research chief John Varley and to technical writer Paul Schullery for their insight and patience over the years. In addition, appreciation is accorded the Yellowstone Institute, Northern Rockies Conservation Cooperative based in Jackson, Wyoming, Teton Science School, and the Greater Yellowstone Coalition. Without the help of all of these people and institutions, completion of the book would not have been possible. For a list of additional sources, please see the bibliography.

Foreword

Yellowstone Wildlife is that most valued of books–a work that is informal, yet informative. I'm most impressed with writer Todd Wilkinson's treatment of his subject. I have been privileged to see Mike Francis's work both at Yellowstone and elsewhere, and his photos are a worthy complement to the excellent text.

Yellowstone National Park has the most remarkable diversity of major mammals in one place within the 48 contiguous states. This variety, and its obvious attraction for the visiting public, also carries a special burden. The public is seldom exposed to such a stunning array of large animals, and has little understanding of how to appreciate them without placing either animals or people in danger.

Although I know that ensuring safety is not one of this handbook's principal aims, I'm impressed with the effective way a message of human safety and wildlife protection is interwoven with the discussion of where and how to enjoy the best wildlife watching opportunities in Yellowstone.

I know that the book will find an enthusiastic audience.

James Ridenour
Director
National Park Service

YELLOWSTON

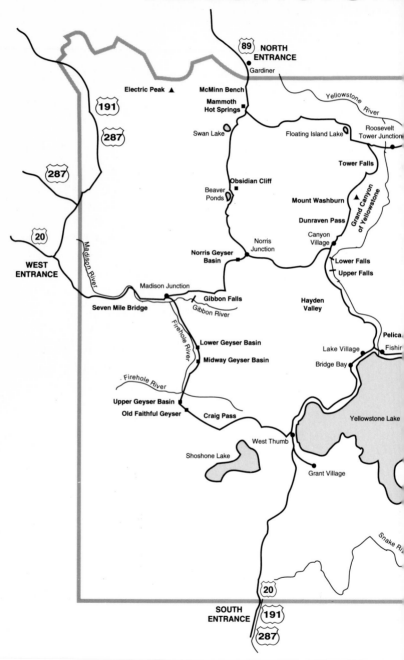

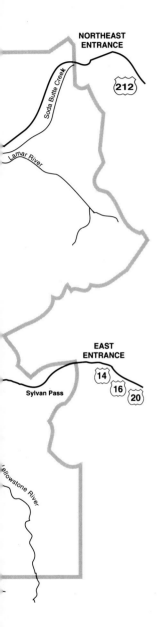

After reading
the "Where to Find"
paragraph in each species
entry, refer to this map
to locate spots where you're
likely to see the animal.

There are six visitor
centers in Yellowstone.
Park rangers can offer
current information about
finding animals on any
given day, and they're
committed to enhancing
your experience in
Yellowstone.

Studying this map
and guide can help you
quickly locate the terrain
and wildlife you hope to see.

Introduction

Watching Yellowstone Wildlife
Be Patient, Listen, and Wait

John Muir, the father of American conservation, came to Yellowstone at the dawn of a new century, via a mode of transportation that today seems unfathomable. Touring the scenery from a horse-drawn carriage, Muir experienced the park differently than do those millions of people who pass through Yellowstone today.

Fortunately, he did not have to try to absorb the park's timeless beauty from a motor home that flashed through at 45 miles per hour. His journey was slow, and the roads were rutted and bumpy, but the wildlife watching was magnificent. Muir saw the real denizens of America's first national park–the feathered and furry inhabitants–because he took his time.

On the shores of Yellowstone Lake, he paused and identified multitudes of birds and animals that wandered out of the forest to find comfort in the water and the gentle breeze. Now, as we visit Yellowstone at the end of the same century, we can marvel at the fact that little has changed.

Yellowstone contains the largest concentration of large and small mammals in the lower 48 states. It is one of the richest wildlife laboratories on earth. Each of us, when turned loose to roam, can become a scientist learning more about animal behavior.

As an ecosystem shaped by natural elements–topography, water, and climate–the park provides visitors with an opportunity to witness animals on an intimate level. Over 370 miles of paved roadway exist to guide travelers across 2.2 million acres–3,500 square miles–a land mass that would cover the combined area of Rhode Island and Delaware.

From practically any vantage point along the Yellowstone highway, there are windows into wildlife habitat that bring extraordinary rewards for people willing to peer inside. A grizzly bear lumbering through a meadow at sunset; a trumpeter swan gliding across a glass-like pond; a bull elk bugling in the mist of autumn; or a bison whose appearance recalls the flavor of primeval America.

Because of cutbacks in the National Park Service's budget, there are fewer rangers along the roadside to assist visitors in locating favorite species. Today, those who are best informed have the best opportunities for seeing wildlife.

This book can become a valuable companion on your expedition into Yellowstone. Remember four basic tenets. First, learn to identify the habitat, because it provides clues about the wildlife likely to be present in a given area. Second, be cognizant of the time of day, and recognize that the productive times for seeing many animals are dawn and dusk. Third, use this book to help you find the species you're looking for. And fourth, when you arrive at a choice location, tune up your senses. Like Muir, be patient, listen, and wait. You will be amply rewarded.

How to Use the Wildlife Watcher's Guide

In this book you'll find vignettes organized by species, covering many of the large birds and animals that reside in Yellowstone. Each section is intended to supply the wildlife viewer with a general sense of what the animal does and where it lives. Following each narrative, there's a brief "Where to Find" paragraph. To locate a species, read this paragraph and check the park map we've provided. Color photographs are also provided to give you a better idea of how the species appears within its natural habitat.

Many of the entries are written with animal feeding habits in mind. Wherever you travel in Yellowstone, the search for food among large and small critters alike is what drives wildlife behavior. So, if you know where the animal feeds, your chances of spotting that animal are greatly enhanced.

Between them, photographer Mike Francis and author Todd Wilkinson have spent more than two decades watching wildlife in Yellowstone. While this book can't guarantee that a visitor will see a given species on each visit to the national park, it is the most informative book on the market, and using it ensures that motorists will be able to find and identify animals on a regular basis. If you have comments or suggestions for future editions of this guide, please send them to NorthWord Press, P.O. Box 1360, Minocqua, WI 54548.

A Wildlife Watcher's Code of Conduct

As a national park, Yellowstone is the domain of wildlife. Humans are guests. The ethics of responsible wildlife watching should always be observed, but they become even more important during the winter months, when animals are strained by the bitter cold and the lack of available food. The elk and bison you see along the roadside in winter are living off limited fat reserves that are crucial if the animal is to survive until spring. By approaching a roadside critter and spooking it into fleeing, you may be hastening the animal's death. But no matter what the time of year in Yellowstone, one should adhere to a few basic principles:

➤ If an animal must change its behavior due to your presence, you're probably too close. If you feel compelled to capture a closer glimpse of a wild animal along the roadside, enlist the help of binoculars, a spotting scope, or a long camera lens. Remember, the chances of a harmful encounter with an animal increase exponentially as you move closer.

➤ Unlike animals in the zoo, Yellowstone's residents are dependent on natural food for survival. Tossing your dinner table scraps in the direction of an animal is a gesture that may have serious consequences. Animals that come to rely on humans for handouts may someday attack an unsuspecting visitor whom they view as a food source, or may starve when all the visitors have gone home and there is no one left to feed them.

➤ Never approach bird nests, because human scent encourages abandonment of the nest by adult birds and predation by coyotes and other omnivores.

➤ Pets, particularly barking dogs, are a liability. They can affect wildlife watching because their commotion is likely to frighten the animals you're trying to spot. It's poor manners to let your pet out of the car where other people are watching wildlife. In Yellowstone, every domestic animal must be under the owner's control and on a leash at all times.

Tips for Watchers

➤ Since the majority of wildlife species in Yellowstone are nocturnal (night foraging) or crepuscular (most active at first and last light), morning and late afternoon are good times for planning a visual safari. At high noon, your prospects are at their poorest. However, if your vacation plans dictate that Yellowstone can only be viewed from the confines of your vehicle at midday, a drive through Hayden Valley is the surest way to find larger animals such as bison.

➤ Travelers in Yellowstone may not realize that their vehicle can provide an effective blind for wildlife watching. Because three million people tour the national park annually, most species have become accustomed to human vehicles. They're often less spooked by a car than by a two-legged intruder. With large and sometimes dangerous critters like bears, bison, and moose omnipresent, a car provides a protective shield as well as an inobtrusive vantage point.

➤ If your visit to Yellowstone can last only a day or even a few hours, there are places in the park where you can quickly find wildlife. The park roadway system is fashioned like a figure eight, with the lower and upper loop sharing the road from Norris Junction to Canyon as a common thread. Each loop crosses different terrain and presents different wildlife habitats. Studying this guide beforehand can help you locate the terrain and wildlife you hope to see.

➤ There are six visitor centers in Yellowstone. Park rangers can offer the best advice for finding animals on any given day, and they're committed to enhancing your experience in Yellowstone. But as experts trained in understanding the dynamics of habitat, they're also committed to protecting the wildlife. According to rangers, a troubling trend has emerged in the past few decades. The majority of animal attacks on humans have involved wildlife watchers who insist upon recording their Yellowstone adventure with close-up photographs of animals. Many attacks have occurred when tourists attempt to pose with wildlife. Remember that animals are not objects that can be photographed with impunity.

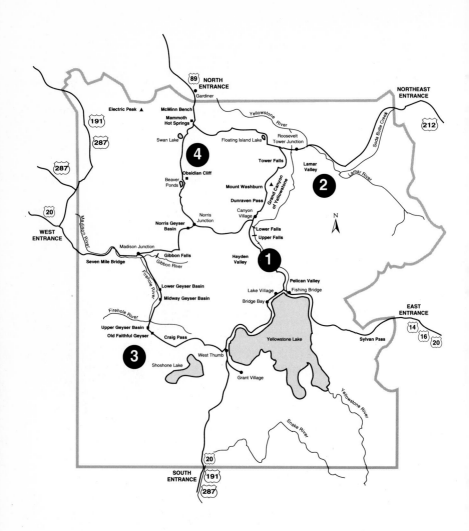

1 .... **Hayden Valley to Yellowstone Lake**
2 .... **Lamar Valley**
3 .... **Upper Geyser Basin to Madison River**
4 .... **Obsidian Cliff to Blacktail Butte**

Welcome to Yellowstone

There are five entrances to Yellowstone National Park. Once you're inside, the route you take determines the type of wildlife and terrain you'll see. To simplify your options, we've pinpointed four regions of the park.

1. The Hayden Valley to Yellowstone Lake region. Wherever you find water in Yellowstone, you're bound to find wildlife. Yellowstone Lake is one of the largest high-altitude bodies of water in the world, with over 136 square miles of surface area surrounded by 110 miles of shoreline. Park highways wind around most of the western and northern portions of the lake. The highway also follows the Yellowstone River, which is the lake's major outlet.

Dissected by the river, Hayden Valley is the premier area for viewing wildlife in Yellowstone. Terrestrial wildlife and waterfowl abound. Along the highway, there are special wildlife viewing areas that explain which species are present. Come here to see bison, coyotes, grizzly bears, American white pelicans, bald eagles, and trumpeter swans.

The northern shores of Yellowstone Lake, from Fishing Bridge east to Steamboat Point, have similar flourishing animal populations in spring and summer. Grizzly bears, bison, moose, mule deer, trumpeter swans, pelicans, and river otters are frequent visitors to the lake.

From Fishing Bridge south to Grant Village, visitors encounter dramatically different landscapes. The rocky lake shores between Bridge Bay and Grant Village attract species including American white pelicans, trumpeter swans, river otters, pine martens, grizzly bears, and the occasional mule deer.

2. Lamar Valley. The northern range of Yellowstone is often compared to Africa's famed Serengeti Plain. Part of the northern range sprawls across Lamar Valley, where large quadrupeds abound. Not only is this area excellent for finding animals, but it's serene and less crowded than Hayden Valley. In winter, Yellowstone's largest elk herd ranges across this intersection of rolling hills and sagebrush savannah. Bison, mule deer, coyotes, badgers, mountain lions, golden eagles, bald eagles, and red-tailed hawks also use the Lamar River as a migration corridor.

3. Upper Geyser Basin near Old Faithful to the Madison River. Set in a backdrop of geysers, hot springs, and fumarole (volcanic openings spewing smoke and gas), this section of the park is astounding. Most of the park's 10,000 thermal features flank the highway, attracting a wide range of wildlife.

During the spring, elk and bison use the forested meadows as calving grounds; grizzly bears feast upon animals that are casualties of winter; and sandhill cranes scan the moist grasslands for grub. During the winter, hot underground water drains into the Firehole River, which then feeds the Madison River. The tepid flows prevent the rivers from freezing over, and the running water attracts trumpeter swans and bald eagles that scrounge for aquatic plants and fish. Weakened bison and elk are common here also.

4. Obsidian Cliff To Blacktail Butte. This drive, which includes Mammoth Hot Springs, is a rich reservoir for birds and animals. As the highway heads north from Obsidian Cliff to Swan Lake, you'll notice the marshy banks of Beaver Ponds, Obsidian Creek, and Indian Creek to the west. Moose, elk, deer, trumpeter swans, coyotes, and occasional grizzly bears are present.

At Mammoth Hot Springs, a resident population of elk is usually visible, and during autumn the bulls begin bugling in their search for mates. From Mammoth eastward across the Blacktail Plateau, you'll see coyotes, deer, and (during the winter months) bison and elk.

From Mammoth north to the park entrance at Gardiner, antelope, bighorn sheep, and mule deer can be seen grazing atop the cliffs and natural benches.

Wildlife Encounters

Here's a chart that estimates the likelihood of encountering wildlife species in Yellowstone. You may want to check off each species that you're able to spot in the park.

COMMON: On any given day, you should encounter one or more of this species.

IRREGULAR: By simply driving through the park without any information, you may see the species on chance encounters. However, by using the tips and suggested locations in this book, you have a good chance of seeing the animal.

RARE: While these animals have been seen in Yellowstone, they are viewed so rarely that it's impossible to predict whether you'll have a roadside encounter.

MAMMALS	COMMON	IRREGULAR	RARE
Grizzly Bear		X	
Black Bear		X	
Bison (Buffalo)	X		
Moose		X	
Elk (Wapiti)	X		
Mule Deer	X		
White-tailed Deer			X
Bighorn Sheep		X	
Mountain Goat			X
Pronghorn (Antelope)	X		
Gray Wolf			X
Coyote	X		
Red Fox			X
Mountain Lion			X
Bobcat			X
Lynx			X
Porcupine		X	
Wolverine			X
Badger		X	
River Otter		X	
Pine Marten		X	
Fisher			X
Mink		X	

MAMMALS	COMMON	IRREGULAR	RARE
Weasel		X	
Beaver		X	
Muskrat		X	
Snowshoe Hare		X	
Uinta Ground Squirrel	X		
Red Squirrel	X		
Marmot	X		
Pika	X		
Least Chipmunk	X		
Yellow-pine Chipmunk	X		

BIRDS	COMMON	IRREGULAR	RARE
Bald Eagle		X	
Golden Eagle			X
Osprey	X		
Peregrine Falcon			X
Red-tailed Hawk	X		
Great Gray Owl		X	
American White Pelican		X	
Trumpeter Swan		X	
Great Blue Heron		X	
Sandhill Crane		X	
Whooping Crane			X
Canada Goose	X		
Harlequin Duck			X
Common Raven	X		
Ruffed Grouse		X	
Blue Grouse		X	

MAMMALS

The GRIZZLY BEAR
Guardian of the Wilderness

In the lower 48 states, no mammal species is more daunting than the grizzly bear. Large, nocturnal, and rare, the grizzly embodies the primeval wilderness, and its mere presence is enough to make human hearts palpitate.

As powerful predators, grizzlies are often viewed as man's fiercest rival. They can outsprint a horse, and they weigh as much as 1,000 pounds. Yet sadly, the advance of human civilization into bear range has spared less than two percent of the animal's former territory. The scarcity of grizzlies has heightened public concern about the great bear's survival.

In 1975 the grizzly was formally listed as a "threatened" species under the Endangered Species Act. Interpreted as a warning by scientists, the classification meant that if drastic action was not taken to protect bear habitat and reduce the number of bear deaths in the lower 48 states, the species would soon become extinct.

The Yellowstone ecosystem is one of only two geographical regions south of Canada where grizzlies have managed to survive in viable numbers. Federal scientists place the Yellowstone population at no less than 250 bears in the park and surrounding national forests.

Bear management today is dramatically different than it was when grizzlies were common roadside attractions. To promote a more natural environment, the national park closed its open-pit dumps and steered bears away from human food to more natural staples, such as young elk, trout, bison carrion, pine nuts, grasses, roots, and berries. While fewer bruins inhabit the roadside as a result, the opportunities for seeing grizzlies are still abundant for those with solid understanding of bear behavior and a little luck.

Grizzly bears are omnivores, meaning that they eat both meat and plants. In fact, they're the second-largest omnivores in North America (dwarfed only by the polar bear). When taxonomists first encountered grizzlies during the 19th century, the bear's brawny size and aggressiveness no doubt inspired its scientific name, *Ursus arctos horribillis*. The common name *Ursus arctos* came later, when taxonomists recognized that grizzlies were the same as European brown bears. While grizzlies can indeed be dangerous if approached too closely, to suggest they are horrible discounts their rightful place as guardians of the wilderness.

Wildlife watchers should look for certain physical characteristics to help distinguish grizzlies from black bears. Grizzlies are generally larger, both in girth and weight. Males, called boars, can attain weights of 1,000 pounds, while females, known as sows, reach about 600 pounds.

The hue of a grizzly's coat may range from tawny cinnamon to light brown or even black. Some grizzlies are flecked with recognizable "silver tips," creating a "grizzled" look that is partially responsible for the bear's name. A feature associated with grizzlies is the shoulder hump, which actually is an area of well-defined muscle used to dig for rodents, insects, and plants. Another trademark is the grizzly's dish-shaped face.

During the long winter months in Yellowstone, grizzlies hibernate in underground dens, where mother bears give birth to their cubs. Hibernation, a process synonymous with sleep, enables bears to live off fat deposits acquired during the spring, summer, and autumn. Bears have a unique adaptation when it comes to pregnancy. While breeding between boars and sows occurs in early summer, a female is able to delay development of the fetus for several months, until she has begun hibernating in the den. During the time of winter sleepiness, the fertilized egg grows in the mother's womb over a gestation period of 45 to 60 days. Although a sow may show no sign of pregnancy in late autumn, she emerges in the spring with a brood of one to three cubs.

Emerging from their dens in late March, solitary males are the first to wake from hibernation. Sows, emerging later, are very protective of their cubs, and will not hesitate to charge intruders whom they think are threatening their babies. This behavioral trait, perhaps more than any other, accounts for dangerous human encounters with bears in Yellowstone.

According to park rangers, no wildlife question is asked more frequently than, "Where are the bears?" The second most common question may be, "How many people are attacked and killed by bears in Yellowstone each year?"

Statistics indicate that during the park's first hundred years (1872 to 1972), fewer than a dozen people were fatally mauled by bears, though scores were injured when they ventured too close to foraging bears or females with cubs. Never, under any circumstances, should you approach a grizzly bear.

The trick to locating and safely viewing bears along the roadside is to consider several factors—the time of day, the type of habitat, and the tools you carry.

Successful nature photographers report that the twilight hours of early morning and late evening offer the best opportunities for seeing grizzlies. During these hours, grizzlies move to "the fringe" between woodlands and meadows, where they scavenge for natural snacks including elk calves. At areas specified, scan the edges of the timber. Notice that each is near a good source of water—a river, marsh, or lake—that is also used by other wildlife.

Seeing a grizzly requires patience and a keen eye. As spring moves into summer and early autumn, grizzlies migrate into the high country, and they may occasionally be seen above the timber line in evaporating snow fields. At each of the locations cited in this book, visitors may be able to spot a grizzly with the naked eye. A tripod will help steady your scope or camera, if you use one.

Near some roadside locations, you may find evidence that a grizzly traveled through the area prior to your arrival. Bear scat (feces) resembles the human variety, and provides hints about what the animals are eating. If you investigate bear scat in the spring, you may find evidence that bears have been consuming spawning trout or carrion from winter-killed elk, bison, and deer. During summer and autumn, bears feed on berries, plant roots, whitebark pine nuts, and insects.

Among the other indicators of grizzly presence are paw prints. All members of the bear family are plantigrade, meaning that they walk on the flats of their feet instead of walking on their toes. Due to their weight, grizzlies may

leave behind an indented print in the mud or snow, which outlines their paw and front claws. Like humans, grizzlies have five toes, though the biggest toe lies on the outside of the foot, not on the inside. If you see a grizzly, report the sighting to a ranger. The information may be useful to biologists who are tracking the movement of bears around the park. Try to notice, if you can, whether the animal is wearing a radio collar. Approximately one of every five bears in Yellowstone has been equipped with a collar that can be tracked via radio telemetry. The collars enable biologists to learn more about bear behavior, and will ultimately help us undertake measures to ensure the survival of the species.

Park your vehicle only at designated turnoffs, and observe the normal etiquette of safe driving. To repeat what was said earlier, never approach grizzly bears. Allow them to pursue their normal activities, and you will thereby learn far more about them than if you forced them to react to your approach.

Where to Find Grizzly Bears

Here are several suggested locations:

➤ Along Dunraven Pass from Canyon Village north past Mt. Washburn and toward the Tower-Roosevelt Area. Just off the northern slope of 8,850-foot Dunraven Pass, north of the near Chittenden Road turnoff overlooking the Antelope Creek drainage. Antelope Creek is closed to all hiking, so it can provide an undisturbed refuge for bears. The result is that the road offers what many consider to be the best vantage point for finding bears in Yellowstone during the late spring, summer, and early autumn months. When bears attract crowds, park rangers attend to the scene to restrain eager photographers and potential bear feeders, and to offer helpful information.

➤ Along the Yellowstone River from its outlet at Yellowstone Lake (near Fishing Bridge) north into Hayden Valley, the site during ancient times of a giant lake bed. Once you arrive in the open expanse of Hayden Valley, watch for overlooks on the east side of the highway and try to locate bears wandering across the undulating meadows as far back as the treeline. Dawns in early summer are the best times.

➤ Lamar Valley. From the Roosevelt developed area east toward the park's northeast entrance at Cooke City, Montana, wildlife watchers can find ideal habitat for grizzlies and for other large mammals. Here, the Lamar River meanders in close proximity to the roadside. Be alert as you watch for bears in the river bottom, and near the treeline across the river.

➤ The east park entrance and the southern tip of Yellowstone Lake's West Thumb. Many grizzlies are spotted near the east park in the spring and fall, while regular reports emerge of grizzly sightings near the Grant Village development during the late spring and early summer, as cutthroat trout spawn in streams that flow into Yellowstone Lake.

The BLACK BEAR
America's Bruin

The black bear's scientific and Latin name, *Ursus americanus,* means "American bear." But many of Yellowstone's visitors look upon the black bruin as "the little brother of the grizzly." Although both species of bears are endemic to Yellowstone, they are different in appearance, size, and behavior. Black bears are the most prolific member of the bear family in North America, and are found from the Pacific coast to the Atlantic seaboard.

Yellowstone is known worldwide as a sanctuary for these popular quadrupeds. According to loose estimates, 650 black bears inhabit the park, outnumbering grizzlies by a three-to-one margin. Surprisingly little is known about black bears, however, because most field studies to date have focused on the threatened grizzlies.

Compared to grizzlies, black bears are docile, though males (boars) and females (sows) have been known to attack humans who accidentally stumble upon a cache of food or wander too close to bear cubs. The biggest mistake made by visitors lies in believing that the bears are tame. Accident reports prove otherwise. Feeding bears is not only dangerous, it encourages animals to forsake natural food for human handouts, a habit that has resulted in human injury and the resultant forced destruction of many bruins. Feeding them just once trains them to seek human foods by hanging around roads, where they may get killed by cars or become aggressive, possibly injuring someone. From 1931 to 1969, an average of 46 people were injured annually by bears in the park, and an average of 24 bears were killed each year.

The primary misconception about black bears is that all of them are black. Depending upon genetic makeup, the shades of their coats can be reddish-tan, blond, chocolate brown, or jet black. Brown-colored black bears are often mistaken for small grizzlies. The size of black bears can generally help establish the difference. Adult boars weigh between 200 and 600 pounds, while sows weigh between 150 and 400 pounds.

Of course, there are other differences. A black bear's rump is higher than its shoulder hump and it will have a "Roman nose," instead of the grizzly's dish-shaped face. Scat from a black bear is tube-shaped, and smaller than grizzly scat.

Tracks reflect the black bear's classification as a plantigrade, or flat-footed walker. The front and rear paw prints look almost human, with five toes, and the paws usually leave a near-to-full-foot impression, shallower in front but deeper in back.

Having adapted to forests over thousands of years, black bears are adept at climbing trees. These escape routes are often used by imperiled cubs. Grizzlies, encumbered by long claws, are not as skilled at ascending Yellowstone's tall but skinny conifers.

Less reliant on brute strength than grizzlies, black bears prey less often upon large game animals, instead employing superb scavenging techniques. During the seven or eight months prior to winter denning, they consume a variety of succulent grasses, roots, berries, and other plants, while eating small rodents, animal carcasses, and elk calves when available.

The black bear's roving nature takes it into open meadows, where the food selection is best. By happy coincidence, this terrain accommodates wildlife watchers who look for bears from the road. The forest fires of 1988 affected a large section of terrain along park roads, and it's conceivable that bear sightings may increase in the burned drainages that have experienced vegetation and rodent invasions. Scientists remain uncertain about habitat overlap between black bears and grizzlies, and are unsure whether the two species compete for territory in the park.

Because their threatened status affords grizzlies federal protection, the more abundant black bears have become increasingly vulnerable to illegal killing, and the poachers acknowledge no boundaries. The bears are slaughtered for gall bladders, paws, and claws, and local populations across the country have been severely diminished by poachers. Fortunately, because of the isolation of Yellowstone's backcountry and diligent ranger patrols, black bears here are less of a target.

Where to Find Black Bears

Visit the Blacktail Plateau region between Mammoth Hot Springs and Tower Roosevelt Junction, and scan meadows between Tower and Antelope Creek south of Tower Falls.

The region between Undine Falls and Floating Island Lake on the Mammoth to Roosevelt Junction should be considered for possible bear-watching excursions by auto, as should the river floodplain of the Gardiner River south and east of Mammoth Hot Springs. Sightings are also frequent south of Roosevelt for several miles past Tower Falls.

Perhaps the best strategy for finding a bear is to stop at park visitor centers and obtain the latest information from rangers. If you spot a bear on the road, report it to the rangers, because the information may help rangers protect the animal from harassment or feeding.

The GRAY WOLF
Predator from the Pleistocene

Will wolves return to Yellowstone? As of this writing, it's a tantalizing question.

Ironically, the U.S. government is currently in a position to decide whether humans should make amends to a species we eradicated from the western states some 60 years ago. And since Yellowstone has demonstrated its leadership as a sanctuary for many imperiled species, we may see the park again make conservation history by restoring wolves.

By the end of the 1930s, federal hunters had succeeded in exterminating the last of the wolves from Yellowstone, apparently writing the final chapter on a predator that had lived in the region for millenia–dating back to the Pleistocene Era, when woolly mammoths and saber-toothed tigers also flourished. In the course of only a few decades, with the use of traps, poisons, and guns, all traces of *Canis lupus* were gone, because ranchers outside the park wanted protection for their cattle and sheep, and park managers worried that wolves were overrunning other species of wildlife. Dozens of recent studies, however, assert that wolves would help restore harmony to one of the greatest wild ecosystems in the temperate zone.

The gray wolf is the largest of canine predators, and is identical to the wolf that inhabits parts of Canada and the northern sections of Minnesota, Wisconsin, and Michigan. Gray wolves weigh between 50 and 130 pounds and use dens to pup, but they do not hibernate. Despite myths and fairytales that attribute "evil" or vicious characteristics to wolves, there has never been a documented case in which a healthy wild wolf has attacked and killed a person in North America. Wild wolves, in fact, prefer to stay away from humans whenever possible.

Attitudes toward wolves are changing, and prominent global zoologists say the wolf's role as predator is important to the proper functioning of natural systems.

Very few national parks have managed to maintain the full complement of native fauna that existed prior to the arrival of Europeans on the continent, but only the absence of wolves prevents Yellowstone from achieving such historical completeness. If wolves return, park officials say the predator will help regulate herds of elk, bison, and deer, populations of which have fluctuated widely.

The Northern Rocky Mountain Wolf Recovery Plan, a monumental biological proposition approved by the U.S. Fish and Wildlife Service in 1987, offers a framework for restoration of wolves to Yellowstone. Funding to draft a working plan and to prepare an Environmental Impact Statement was given to the Fish and Wildlife Service and the National Park Service by Congress in fiscal year 1992, with a directive to complete the environmental review within 18 months. If the review recommends that humans bring wolves back artificially, the predators could be returned by the end of the 20th century.

There is much evidence indicating that if wolves are not artificially returned to Yellowstone by federal biologists, the wolves may accomplish the task themselves. It's clear that wolves from Canada are immigrating into northwestern Montana, the Idaho panhandle, and northeastern Washington. How long it will be before gray wolves re-establish a toehold in Yellowstone is a matter of speculation.

Where to Find Gray Wolves

While wolves do not officially exist in the national park, Yellowstone's northern range–home to one of the largest elk herds in the lower 48 states–could become the first place where transplanted animals are released. In terms of setting, climate, and prey base, the Lamar Valley constitutes the finest habitat for wolves outside of Canada and Alaska.

People around the Yellowstone area have reported seeing canines that they believe are wolves, though actual pack activity has not been verified to date.

Because wolves are mobile creatures that range widely, the possibility that lone animals pass through the national park certainly exists.

Visitors who would like more information on wolves in Yellowstone can write: Yellowstone Research Office, P.O. Box 168, Yellowstone National Park, WY 82190.

The COYOTE
Singing Trickster

Called "the trickster" by native Americans, coyotes (*Canis latrans*) are currently top dog in Yellowstone Park. Having survived the same extermination campaigns that eliminated wolves from the park between 1910 and 1930, coyotes have by default become the predominant canid predator, though their role in wild ecosystems is often overlooked.

Intelligent and social animals, coyotes grow as large as a medium-sized dog. Their fur color varies according to habitat, though in Yellowstone the majority of adults have grizzled gray coats with a whitish underbelly, bushy tail, and reddish hair on the front and back legs. On the average, coyotes weigh between 30 and 40 pounds, about half as much as a wolf. In telling the two species apart, it's helpful to remember that coyotes are comparatively dainty. Their noses, heads, legs, and feet are less prominent. Wolves have broader muzzles, massive heads, long legs, and huge feet.

The coyote is a rover, seeming always to be on the move. It's normal for small groups of coyotes to amble dozens of miles during a night of hunting. When in pursuit of a rabbit or rodent, they can sprint at speeds of 35 to 40 miles per hour. Like wolves, coyotes are pack animals that work together to bring down young deer, pronghorn, elk calves, or other winter-weakened prey.

An interesting behavioral trait, observed in Yellowstone, is that a coyote will accompany a badger. As the badger plows through the den of a ground squirrel or marmot, the coyote will opportunistically wait near secondary

escape hatches.

There are many ways to detect coyote presence. First, listen for howls, the famous sound of coyotes "singing." Scan the ground for coyote tracks. Because they walk on the toes of their paws, not on the flat bottoms of their feet, coyotes are considered digitigrade (toe walkers). This is apparent, as each footprint has four toe marks and a heel mark behind.

The management of coyotes in Yellowstone is unusual, simply because the predators are left alone to interact with the wildlife around them. Outside the park, coyotes are regarded as vermin by most cattle and sheep ranchers, who shoot them at will. Studies by Yellowstone researchers indicate that when coyotes are not hunted or killed artificially, their numbers stabilize and the population level generally remains the same year after year. In areas where humans routinely kill them, however, their survival tendency leads them to increase their reproduction of young, which may actually result in higher population densities. The exact number of coyotes in the park is not known, though they are far more abundant than red foxes.

Habituation to human food is regarded as the greatest threat to coyotes, for animals that have been fed will aggressively confront people. Some encounters have been dangerous. In recent episodes, cross country skiers in the Old Faithful area were attacked by hungry coyotes who associated humans with food. Not only were the people bitten, but coyotes were destroyed.

For obvious reasons, then, you should never feed coyotes. The table scraps you leave behind could become a death sentence for a coyote or could result in injury to a human being.

Where to Find Coyotes

Although coyotes are nocturnal in areas where they're persecuted, they do not fear humans in Yellowstone, so they're active at all hours. Look for them year-round in Lamar Valley; on the northern, inland shores of Yellowstone Lake; in the Upper and Lower geyser basins around Old Faithful; in Hayden Valley and across Blacktail Deer Plateau. Watch for them, too, when you're viewing herds of bison, elk, or pronghorns.

During any season, coyotes can be spotted at Yellowstone roadsides. From Lamar Valley to the south park entrance, and from Sylvan Pass to Mammoth Hot Springs, they are common to the middle and lower elevations. If you're driving, pull over, turn off your engine, and sit quietly for a while. Better yet, park and walk to a hilltop. Sit, watch, and listen.

The coyotes of Yellowstone are robust and heavily furred, which means they're often mistaken for wolves. Let a ranger know if you see what you believe may be a wolf.

The RED FOX
Shyest of Predators

Red foxes (*Vulpes vulpes*) are the shyest of the dog-like predators in Yellowstone, and are seldom seen.
Night hunters that prowl the edges of forests, these omnivores trot long distances

over the course of a night, but lie low during the day. The species is found across most of North America, and its "cunning" ability to outwit fox hunters and fur trappers is legendary. More research on the red fox presence in Yellowstone is needed, and visitors will be considered very lucky indeed if they see one. But don't let that prevent you from trying.

Several of the animal's physical characteristics can help wildlife watchers differentiate between foxes and coyotes. An adult fox weighs about 15 pounds, perhaps half the weight of a small adult coyote. Foxes also sport the classic long, slender snout. Unlike wolves and coyotes, foxes rarely howl or sing as a form of gregariousness.

What sets the animal apart, of course, is its coloration. As the name suggests, the typical red fox has orange-red fur, which runs across the top of its body from nose to hindquarters. The fox has a spot of white on the tip of its fluffy black and red tail. The underside of its body, from neck to posterior, is covered by a creamy white fur, and its paws are black. However, some red foxes may be all gray or reddish-blond. As with black bears, red foxes take on hues other than the color for which they're primarily known.

In learning more about foxes, we begin to understand how predators interrelate within a wild ecosystem. The planned restoration of wolves to Yellowstone may benefit red foxes and other animals–including coyotes, wolverines, weasels, martens, eagles, ravens, and magpies–by providing these scavengers with a regular source of carrion during winter months, when other food is difficult to get.

Never, under any circumstances, approach or feed a fox. They will bite if provoked, and they can carry rabies. However, no Yellowstone canid has tested positive for rabies in 120 years.

Where to Find Red Foxes

The timidity of foxes means they're less accessible from the road than coyotes. Sightings are infrequent and seasonal, with most occurring in winter, spring, or autumn around the Canyon Village Development. In meadows that roll away from the Grand Canyon of the Yellowstone, foxes are occasionally spotted from the roadside as they're hunting at dusk and dawn. In early autumn before the frost, foxes may be seen gorging themselves on grasshoppers, which are abundant in meadows north of Canyon Village on the road to Dunraven Pass.

The MOUNTAIN LION
Stealthful Prowler

Sleek. Stealthful. Shrewd. Feared. These words describe one predator in Yellowstone that is known by many names–mountain lion, cougar, puma, catamount. Yet one adjective puts the existence of this remarkable species in perspective–rare.

Mountain lions (*Felis concolor missoulensis*) are the largest members of the cat family to inhabit North America. Weighing between 75 and 200 pounds at adulthood, these tawny carnivores have no natural enemies except humans. Agile and fleet, a mature lion can leap nearly 20 feet in a single bound.

Because of Yellowstone's abundant prey base of elk, deer, bighorn sheep, and small mammals, certain areas of the park (where snow gets no deeper than 20 inches in winter) provide good year-round habitat for a species that routinely roams 20 miles or more in a night of searching for food. The fact that mountain lions are so seldom seen in the wild, however, makes them an enigma when it comes to wildlife watching. Your odds of seeing a mountain lion from the road are significantly poorer than, say, the odds of being struck by lightning.

The explanations are fairly simple. These elusive cats are night hunters. They usually occupy rocky sections of the backcountry, and there is little reason for a mountain lion to venture near developed areas of the park. Never in Yellowstone's recorded history has there been a documented instance in which a mountain lion attacked a person. In fact, few rangers have ever seen one.

The lion's low profile can also be attributed to low numbers. During the first three decades of the 20th century, federal hunters and trappers were hired to eradicate mountain lions and other predators that preyed upon popular park wildlife, such as deer and elk. Mountain lions were spared from complete elimination, and seemed to increase in number during the 1970s and 1980s, but their low productivity and their need for a large range have kept the population low nonetheless. Research has shown that about 20 lions occupy a study area measuring 320 square miles, but there are, no doubt, more in the park during summer. Between 1960 and 1985, almost 300 reliable sightings of mountain lions were reported, most near winter ranges for elk.

Signs of a mountain lion include copious scat ranging from dark spheres to pellets, often with traces of whatever the lion ingested, such as elk hair or bones. The tracks are wider than they are long, and four-toed like those of a housecat but larger. Moving in front paw/back paw pairs, the impressions are staggered, with front pawprints overlapping those of the hind paw. The prints measure between 3 and 4 inches, and show no claw mark because the claws are retracted when walking. Although humans are their only natural enemy, these cats will tangle with coyotes in winters when food is in short supply. In more populated parts of the Rockies, lions have attacked children.

The safest spot from which to view a mountain lion is the inside of your vehicle.

Where to Find Mountain Lions

It's improbable that you will see mountain lions from the roadside. However, sightings of mountain lions have been becoming more frequent in Yellowstone's Lamar Valley and along the Yellowstone, Madison, and Gallatin river drainages in recent years. Specifically, sightings have been reported along the park highway east of Lamar Valley and the highway over Sylvan Pass, and in the Tower-Roosevelt Junction area.

The BOBCAT
One Scarce Cat

Bobcats are a mysterious presence in Yellowstone. Little is known about their exact numbers or their distribution within the ecosystem. Bobcats (*Felis rufus*) do roam the alpine forests of the 2.2 million-acre park, but in small numbers.

An abundant smorgasbord of rabbits, small rodents, and birds is available in the park to sustain the cats, and irregular sightings on adjacent national forests confirm that a few of these omnivorous felines spend at least part of the year here. But why are these tree-climbing predators so scarce?

In Yellowstone, the scarcity may simply be due to park habitat. Bobcats, like mountain lions, must occupy rocky, wind-blown or south-facing slopes at lower elevations–habitat that is limited in Yellowstone.

Since the early 19th century, bobcats were trapped heavily by fur traders, which caused local extinctions. There is still a hunting season on bobcats in the states surrounding Yellowstone, and the wilderness terrain in which the cats thrive has been continually destroyed in areas outside the park. But these factors may have only cursory implications when compared to the habitat requirements of the animal itself.

The bobcat is native only to the lower 48 states and southern areas of

Canada. It may be further limited to areas of little snow, as are mountain lions, where total accumulation is 20 inches or less.

Bobcats survive by stealthily stalking their prey at night. Except for humans and occasional skirmishes with lions, coyotes, or wolves, the bobcat has no known enemies. Although it's improbable that wildlife watchers will see bobcats from the roadside, here are a few tips to aid you in making identifications.

Bobcats are so named for their knobby, bobbed tails. While the coat of a bobcat is conspicuous–changing subtly from tawny brown in warm months to grayish in winter–the distinguishing marks of this woodland cat are the many leopard-like black spots that flank its sides and legs. The outer flanks of its underbelly are mottled, while the center of the belly is white or a creamy color. A bobcat's face has irregular black stripes, and the tail sports a black ring that is broken by white on the underside.

Like canine predators, bobcats travel vast ranges in search of food. Given the animal's dependence on food sources that can decrease due to drought, harsh winters, and the marginal habitat in Yellowstone, the number of bobcats has probably never been high in the park.

Where to Find Bobcats

Sightings of bobcats have been most frequent in the northeast corner of the park, and over Sylvan Pass between Fishing Bridge and the park's east entrance. There have also been sightings just inside the park's south entrance. Report all suspected sightings to a ranger. The information is helpful and could ultimately result in better protection of the species.

The LYNX
Cat of Many Continents

Lynx (*Felis canadensis*) are deep-snow, sub-alpine forest creatures, equipped with snowshoe-like paws. Very little habitat within Yellowstone is ideal for the lynx, but occasional sightings indicate that a few roam the park.

Like the bobcat, the lynx was eagerly sought by fur traders, suffering as a result from local extinctions. The lynx is now a protected species in Wyoming and Idaho, but destruction of wilderness habitat continues to influence its presence outside of Yellowstone.

The lynx is a widespread animal, found in parts of Africa, Asia, and Europe, and common in Canada and Alaska, though the southern tip of its North American territory extends only to the U.S.-Canadian border and slightly down the spine of the Rockies. Yellowstone, then, is about as far south as the lynx ventures on this continent.

A furtive prowler, the lynx is a wide-ranging nighttime hunter whose preda-tory habits parallel those of the mountain lion and the bobcat. It has no known enemies, although it may have unpleasant or competitive encounters from time to time with people, lions, coyotes, or wolves.

The lynx has a short tail that is ringed by alternating bands of color. The cat's long, silky coat is gray-buffed, sometimes augmented by blotches of brown on its belly. There's a tuft of hair that is striped black under the lynx's chin. The width of its paws, which are furred between and around the pads, allows the lynx to race across snow in pursuit of prey and approach without much sound. In many areas, the lynx population parallels that of one of its favorite meals, the snowshoe hare. When snowshoe numbers decline every decade or so, the lynx population dips similarly.

To help the park protect its lynx, report all suspected sightings to a ranger. Young lynx resemble cuddly domestic kittens, but if you should happen to encounter them, do not approach. A mother lynx will fight ferociously to pro-tect her young.

Where to Find Lynx

Within Yellowstone, lynx inhabit essentially the same terrain as bobcats. Though a roadside sighting is quite unlikely, you might spot a lynx in the northeast corner of the park, over Sylvan Pass between Fishing Bridge and the east entrance, or just inside the south entrance.

The BISON (Buffalo)
Our Window to the Past

By the middle 1800s, the population of American bison had already started to decline, from a one-time high of perhaps 60 million animals. Over the next fifty years, widespread throngs of millions were reduced to regional thousands, and the thousands then plummeted to fewer than 50 wild bovines in the entire lower 48 states.

Teetering on the brink of extinction, the last few free-roaming bison in the United States took refuge in a corner of northwest Wyoming known as Yellowstone National Park. The animals you see today along the roadsides in Yellowstone are descendants of those survivors—behemoths from a time when bison, or "buffalo" as they are popularly known, were the largest terrestrial mammals in North America.

The number counted in Yellowstone today is about 2,500, divided into three distinct herds that stretch across the park. The sight of these herbivores grazing across the rolling plateaus brings thoughts of pre-history to mind, when ancestors of these 2,000-pound creatures first crossed the Bering Strait from Eurasia and quickly populated the Great Plains of this continent.

Until the 1950s, the National Park Service operated the "Buffalo Ranch" near Rose Creek in Lamar Valley (now home to the Yellowstone Institute) where bison were carefully husbanded and cropped to ensure growth of the population. The Yellowstone bison (*Bison bison*) has lineage from subspecies that wandered both the northern woods and the plains. Males (called bulls) and females (called cows) have black horns, which are not shed like the antlers of elk, deer, and moose. The bulk of a bison's coat is composed of shaggy, reddish-brown fur, though the head is dark brown. Some animals have dark brown manes and beards. Bulls are larger, standing six feet tall at the shoulder while females grow to five feet.

Docile and seemingly oblivious to activity around them, bison have a calm demeanor, sometimes misinterpreted as an open invitation to approach. They are not, however, domesticated cows in a pasture, but wild creatures that are dangerous to those who invade their privacy. It may surprise some that three times as many humans have been gored by bison since 1980 than the total number of humans attacked by grizzly and black bears combined. Distance should be afforded, especially to lone bulls who have sought seclusion for a reason, or to cows with young calves.

The bison herds are most active in the cool of morning and evening, while the heat of day is usually a time when adults rest and ruminate (chew their cud). Caution: As the flyers distributed at park entrance stations suggest, the 2,000-pound bison use Yellowstone roads in the summer and winter, night and day. Drive with care!

Where to Find Bison

An excursion to Yellowstone is not complete without a drive through Hayden Valley. Here, you may see hundreds of bison flanking the roadway during daylight hours. Young bulls may be sparring, or adults may seek relief from the summer heat in streams that dissect the valley floor. Nearby, you can see bison on the northern shore of Yellowstone Lake, particularly in Pelican Valley east of Fishing Bridge.

Clusters of bison are viewed regularly in the Lower Geyser Basin and the Firehole River drainage, occupied by the Mary Mountain Herd; and in the Lamar Valley along the Lamar River, home of the resident Northern Herd. Both herds have been sources of controversy, because bison from these groups migrate outside of the national park during periods of heavy snow. The state of Montana enlisted hunters and game wardens to shoot and kill wandering bison, because they may carry the disease brucellosis, which can cause abortions in domestic cattle. Park scientists are now developing management strategies that would allow the Yellowstone bison, the largest free-roaming population in the world, to continue to use lands outside the park as a winter range.

The MOOSE
Gentle Giant of the Marshes

As the largest member of the deer family, the moose (*Alces alces shirasi*) is a long-lived, ravenous vegetarian that seems charmingly oversized. Bulls and cows are both covered with a coat of dark brown hair that appears almost black when wet. Their hind legs show a white "wash" at times.

While the imposing, palmate antlers are a trademark of males, both sexes share features that are delightfully pronounced. The elongated snout, bulbous nose, and pendulous dewlap or "bell" under the throat distinguish them from other ungulates (hooved animals) in the ecosystem. Except during mating, bulls are solitary, while cows stand guard over their twin calves until the animals are about a year old.

Next to bison, moose are the largest animals encountered in the park. Healthy bulls and cows can live into their twenties, reach staggering weights of 1,000 pounds or more, and achieve shoulder heights topping seven feet. Compared to other megafauna in Yellowstone, moose are newcomers, immigrating as late as the 1870s into the park from the south, and onto the park's northern range by 1913. About 200 now inhabit the northern range, and perhaps 600 more live elsewhere within the park.

During the summer, moose frequent shallow ponds, marshes, and streams

---

to feed on succulent aquatic plants. Notice that, as they wade through water, moose will dip their nose in halfway to grasp a bite of vegetation. About 90 percent of the moose's winter diet is composed of "browse"–the supple ends of twigs from conifers, willows, and shrubs.

Bulls, particularly during the autumn breeding season, may flay grasses upon their antlers and stomp moodily through the underbrush as a menacing means of displaying masculinity. Like elk and deer, bull moose shed their antlers following the breeding season, which is also known as the rut. Their giant racks help the bulls assert dominance during sparring matches with other males. Later they begin sprouting new, velvet-covered antlers. In late summer, bulls rub the velvet off by grinding and sharpening the pointed tines on trees. This behavior explains why some antler edges have a polished look to them.

Where to Find Moose

The most popular place is Willow Park, a haven for moose between Mammoth Hot Springs and Norris Junction that's a regular stopover for professional wildlife photographers. During the spring, summer and autumn months, you may see moose near Bridge Bay, Lake, and Fishing Bridge along Yellowstone Lake northward into Hayden Valley. Other moose-viewing locations include Phantom Lake northwest of Tower-Roosevelt, and roadside areas near the east and northeastern entrances to the park. Hikers in the Canyon Village and Lake areas frequently encounter cow moose with calves.

The ELK (Wapiti)
September's Brassy Bugler

No other sound in Yellowstone portends the advent of winter like the rapturous wails of bull elk. Witnessing the rut, from the dramatic sparring of bulls locked in combat to the brooding courtship of females, is simply wildlife watching at its finest.

Visitors may encounter elk (*Cervus elaphus nelsoni*) virtually anywhere along the roadside in Yellowstone from April through October. These regal cervids are the most abundant large mammal species in the park, numbering about 31,000 individual animals during the summer. About 21,000 remain in the park through the winter.

The words "elk" and "wapiti" (pronounced WOP-it-tee) are used interchangeably, for they refer to the same species of ungulate, or hooved animal. Wapiti, arguably the more poetic label, is a term handed down from Shawnee Indians that means "white rump," a description that aids in biological identification.

The subspecies of elk inhabiting Yellowstone is known as the Rocky Mountain elk, a massive, widely-distributed animal native to montane forests.

At the end of the 19th century, elk were chiefly an animal of the West, but even then they nearly disappeared from the Rockies, because hunters killed them by the millions to sell their ivory-like teeth and to keep them off agricultural lands used by cattle ranchers.

Yellowstone, with its prohibition on sport hunting, has long served as a valuable reservoir of elk, fueling repopulation efforts in several states surrounding the national park.

Physically, elk are bigger than deer but smaller than a horse. Bulls, adorned by their infamous antlers, achieve average weights ranging between 500 and 1,000 pounds, and stand up to five feet tall at the shoulders. Cows, which bear no antlers, weigh between 400 and 600 pounds. The sexes can be distinguished by looking carefully at their coats. Bulls' coats are lighter, a difference that's especially noticeable during winter.

The elk's head is darkish brown; the body from shoulders to tailbone is tan; and the rump, of course, is creamy white. An elk walks on its hooves, so elk tracks resemble cloven half moons. Droppings take the form of flattened piles similar to cow dung when the elk are eating succulent foods, but change to pellets during the months when they subsist on dry food.

Elk are spread across most of the park's interior during summer. In September and October, the breeding season commences. Bulls emanate high-pitched "bugles," adding a brassy sound to the national park that's as colorful as the changing leaves. Stomping their hooves and wielding antlers in furious combat, bulls demarcate their territory through sparring, and try to gather many cows into their harem. Four to five months later, the antlers are shed and the reproductive cycle begins anew.

It's illegal in Yellowstone to use artificial calls to imitate the bugle of bulls. Although some employ this technique to draw animals closer, numerous photographers have been charged by elk that mistake their calls for those of other wapiti.

In late fall, elk collect into migratory groups. They flow out of Yellowstone on ancient game trails established hundreds or possibly thousands of years ago by their ancestors. In November, Yellowstone's largest elk herd begins to converge on the park's northern range, where as many as 20,000 animals seek vegetation hidden beneath a snowy blanket.

One-fourth of these animals may not survive the winter, but the high mortality rate benefits other animals in the ecosystem, namely bears, coyotes, ravens, and other scavengers that depend on winter-weakened elk as an important supply of protein. Despite their size, elk are the main diet of local mountain lions, and in recent years field biologists have documented grizzlies taking down elk calves.

Cow elk sometimes leave their calves hidden, or in a nursery group with other cows. These calves are not abandoned. You should not approach or touch them, since they have little scent and, if not panicked into running, will normally be safe until the mother elk returns. If the mother returns as you are attempting to fondle her calf, you may find yourself the target of a charging animal.

Where to Find Elk

The park's high-elevation meadows are places to scan from the roadside. Elk congregate regularly along the Gibbon River near Norris Junction, throughout the lodgepole pine forests to Elk Park, and further north at Mammoth Hot Springs. Year-round, wapiti can be seen grazing in sagebrush meadows and on the artificially green lawns around park headquarters at Mammoth Hot Springs.

Keep a careful watch as you travel between Dunraven Pass and Tower Falls, near the Lower and Upper Geyser Basins around Old Faithful, and along the Madison River between the west park entrance and Madison Junction.

Migratory elk herds are also seen in winter and spring along U.S. Highway 191, which passes inside the park between West Yellowstone and Bozeman.

The Firehole River, particularly from the Lower Geyser Basin to Madison Junction, is a favorite spot among wildlife photographers who hope to capture the elk rut in the fall.

The National Elk Refuge in Jackson Hole, Wyoming, is a winter sanctuary for several thousand elk from the Bridger-Teton National Forest as well as Yellowstone and Grand Teton national parks. The elk mass here between November and March each year. Wildlife watchers can take sleigh rides through the wintering herds for a nominal charge, and the proceeds help buy feed for the animals. About a hundred bison also winter here.

The PRONGHORN (Antelope)
Fastest Fauna on Four Feet

Pronghorn (*Antilocapra americana*) are favorites among wildlife watchers in Yellowstone. Although traditional folk songs like "Home, Home on the Range" have immortalized them as "antelope," they are more correctly identified as pronghorn. As relatives of such fleet African species as gazelles, pronghorn are the fastest animals to race across the plains of North America. Capable of reaching speeds of 70 miles per hour for miles at a time, they can also spring 20 feet in a single leap. Their latin genus, *Antilocapra*, means antelope or "goat," indicating that they are remotely related to goats.

The population of pronghorn in the park has fluctuated widely, reaching an all-time high of perhaps 2,000 at the turn of the 19th century, approaching complete extirpation by the 1920s, and numbering about 500 today. In more ways than one, this marvelous population is unique. Because it is cut off from pronghorn breeding groups elsewhere in Montana, Yellowstone's pronghorn population exists on a sort of biological island.

Before settlement brought houses and barbed wire fences to the Yellowstone River drainage, nothing impeded the movement of pronghorn and bison along the river clear across to its confluence with the Missouri River in North Dakota. The animals that reside in north-central Yellowstone Park were merely an extension of countless numbers utilizing the riverside as a key transportation corridor.

When you examine these small, hooved quadrupeds, it becomes obvious why they are called pronghorn. They are handsome creatures whose symmetrical, prong-like horns are striking on males (bucks) and hardly noticeable on females (does). Their brownish markings, combined with a white-streaked underbelly, neck, and rump, make them easy to distinguish from other large mammals in the park.

To tell the sexes apart, look for horns longer than the ears and black hair on the face and neck area of bucks, which are generally taller (about three feet at the shoulder) than females and weigh between 110 and 140 pounds. The horns of does, if you're able to spot them, are shorter than the ears.

The presence of pronghorn in such a small region of Yellowstone demonstrates the diversity of park habitat and the importance of specific niches. Preferring lower elevations and open, sagebrush-savanna, pronghorn occupy terrain that is shared with deer and elk, particularly during winter, when many animals gather on the northern rangeland to share abundant forage and plants.

As late spring and early summer approach, females begin disappearing from view, finding isolated coulees where they give birth to their young, often twins. A seasonal occupation of both sexes is the shedding of a bark-like sheath from their horns. This occurs in late autumn, following breeding.

The prohibition on hunting in the park has helped propagate large bucks that would be coveted by hunters outside the Yellowstone boundary. Occasional forays into private lands and the adjacent national forest make pronghorn subject to hunting, but this involves only a small number of animals each year.

Where to Find Pronghorn

Bands of pronghorn typically congregate year-round at the north park entrance and along the seasonal gravel road running one way between Mammoth and Gardiner. Be on the alert for hikers and mountain bikers on the gravel road. The McMinn Bench area is quite productive for pronghorn watching, and the animals are often visible on the paved road between Yellowstone's stone arch and the open meadows beyond the gate where you pay to enter the park.

The MULE DEER
Black-Tailed Browser

When you drive through Yellowstone, practically everywhere you go is mule deer country.

Nomads of the West, mule deer (*Odocoileus hemionus*) are ideally suited to the rugged slopes of the Rocky Mountains. Although there is no precise count of the mule deer population, "mulies" may number about 3,000 in Yellowstone, ranging over most areas of the national park in summer but migrating to lower elevations outside the park in winter.

Because mule deer are members of the cervid (deer) family, the males (bucks) flaunt symmetrical antlers that are shed late in the winter. The size of antlers is determined by genetic make-up and by the availability of nutrient-rich forage. Females (does) do not grow antlers.

Roadside indications of mule deer include tracks that resemble cloven half moons and range in length from 2 1/2 to 3 1/4 inches, depending upon the deer's size and sex. Other clues include beds of matted grass where mule deer rest during the heat of the day. The pellets of mule deer are similar to those of elk, taking the form of matted piles or dark brown balls.

Given their relative abundance in the greater Yellowstone area today, it's difficult to fathom that mule deer were once reduced to dangerously low

numbers in the region by overhunting. At the turn of the century, the park served as one of the few sanctuaries for the species, and it continues to nurture trophy-sized bucks whose racks are coveted by sport hunters. Harvesting of any animal by hunters is prohibited inside the national park, though some mule deer are shot after leaving Yellowstone in the fall.

Nature has given this plant-eating animal the ability to identify its enemies and flee on a moment's notice. Three features make the mule deer easily recognizable: its oversized, creamy-white ears; its ropy, black-tipped tail; and its unique way of jumping and landing on all four feet at once, a gait called "stotting."

While mule deer bucks are polygamous, they do not amass harems of females like their elk counterparts. Males lead a solitary life except during the rut, while females congregate in groups on the same winter range year after year. This gathering is called "yarding."

The mule deer's physical size and preferred habitat further distinguish it from its smaller relative, the whitetail. The mule deer's coat takes on different shades as the seasons progress. Summer brings a reddish tint, while winter produces a covering flecked with gray that serves as camouflage during the snowy season.

The mule deer's muscular frame reflects the fact that its summer range may include grasslands located on steep summits as high as 10,000 feet. The primary enemies of mule deer in Yellowstone are mountain lions, coyotes, and grizzly bears, which prey on deer calves in spring. If wolves are restored to Yellowstone, they too will undoubtedly make mule deer a staple.

Despite its reputation as a browser, the mule deer's diet is highly complex. Mulies feed in mature Douglas-fir forests, but they are also creatures of the sagebrush flats. Studies have documented mule deer in the Rockies that eat over 673 different species of plants. While less discriminating in their cravings than pronghorn and bighorn sheep, mule deer often embark on foraging expeditions taking them 30 miles or more in a night. They feed on grasses during spring and summer, and on branches of trees and sagebrush-juniper in the winter. Such palatable greens now flourish in many burned sections of Yellowstone following the historic 1988 forest fires.

Where to Find Mule Deer

The Lake, Tower, and Mammoth areas contain mule deer during most of the year. The crepuscular mulies are also seen frequently from the roadside on the south shores of Yellowstone Lake near Grant Village, and on the lake's northern shores from Bridge Bay to Lake Butte. Check also near Old Faithful, and between the northeast entrance of the park and Lamar Valley.

The WHITE-TAILED DEER
Next-Door Neighbor

When we think of North American big game, we often think of the white-tailed deer. Whitetails (*Odocoileus virginianus*) are the most abundant deer species in the lower 48 states, and are found in regions from suburban lawns to the rural woodlands. Yet the popular species is scarce in Yellowstone, and is found chiefly along rivers and streams flanked by deciduous (leaf-bearing) trees, such as cottonwoods and willow thickets.

The whitetail is more gregarious and tolerant of humans than its larger cousin, the mule deer, and the two species are rarely found within the same niche. White-tailed deer are smaller and leaner than mulies, and are distinguished by their reddish-brown coats, white underbellies, and tails that are brown on top but whitish on the inside, like a snowy flag. Male whitetails grow antlers, but females do not.

The whitetail's occupation of Yellowstone has been irregular over the years, and centers on the northern valleys of the park. Here, their range overlaps somewhat with other members of the cervid (deer) family, including mule deer, elk, and antelope. Historically, a small number of whitetails wintered in lowlands near the Gardiner and Yellowstone rivers in the park, but the species was largely extinct in the area by 1930. Biologists believe this extirpation was caused by external factors beyond Yellowstone's borders, including livestock grazing, land clearing and development, and human hunting.

Where to Find White-tailed Deer

Whitetails are frequently spotted in farmer's fields that are 20 miles or less north of the national park, but they are rarely seen within the park itself. The best viewing area for whitetails is a stretch 20 to 30 miles north of Gardiner, Montana, along U.S. Highway 89.

The BIGHORN SHEEP
Heaven Dweller

Defining the niche of bighorn sheep in Yellowstone is an easy task. Finding a sheep near the roadside, however, is not. Bighorns are creatures of the heavens who covet isolated nooks and crags, where they can escape from predators. Few species are better suited to the mountains of Yellowstone, and no other species is so capable of navigating terrain at high altitudes. The Rocky Mountain bighorn sheep (*Ovis canadensis*) is tied inextricably to a kingdom of ceaseless winds and bitter cold.

About 300 bighorns inhabit Yellowstone's northern range, with an unknown number present in the rest of the park's interior. By their appearance alone, bighorns signify ruggedness. Males (rams) are easily identified by the classic C-shaped curl of their horns, while females (ewes) sprout tiny fingers of horn from the tops of their skulls. So subtle are these spikes that bighorn ewes are frequently mistaken for goats. Nimble-footed and built with a low center of gravity, bighorns can scramble across rock walls too steep for most predators and pursuing humans. They disappear in a blink, only to reappear on another cliff, oblivious to the perilous footing. The bighorn is one of several members of the bovid family, which includes bison, mountain goats, and musk oxen. In modern times, though, only sheep and bison have been native to the park.

The biggest threats to the survival of bighorn sheep are human disruption of habitat, predators, and disease. In 1981 and 1982, an epidemic of chlamydia, or pink-eye, swept through the park's bighorn population, leaving hundreds of sheep blinded. Many died as a result, though it appears that bighorn numbers have substantially recovered.

Rams in Yellowstone are renowned for their fully developed horns, a prize coveted by sportsmen and poachers outside the park. In 1987 the state of Montana auctioned a bighorn sheep license. One hunter paid a record $109,000 for the privilege of shooting a ram in an area outside the park. Of course, hunting is not permitted within Yellowstone, but this has not deterred poachers, who enter Yellowstone illegally and kill bighorns that might qualify as trophy animals. Park visitors can play a role in preventing the destruction of bighorns by reporting any suspicious activity to rangers.

Bighorns choose spectacular places to graze, usually within 300 yards of cliffs, and they also raise their young near such sites. Although highly social animals, bighorns usually separate into nursery bands of ewes, lambs, and subadults, while rams form groups among themselves.

Where to Find Bighorn Sheep

If there's any spot where you can almost count on seeing a bighorn sheep (no site affords 100 percent certainty), that location is along the slopes of Mt. Washburn. By late summer, motorists may observe bighorns clambering down the bouldered washes that drain toward the park highway over Dunraven Pass. Here's another promising route: Drive to the parking lot at Chittenden Road on the north side of Dunraven, or to the picnic area at Dunraven Pass, and walk to the manned fire lookout tower on the summit of Mt. Washburn. The sheep have a high tolerance for human hikers, and are readily seen. Remember to stay on the road or trail at all times. This high alpine environment is fragile, and damage to vegetation can be irreparable.

There are other vantages. Armed with binoculars or spotting scopes, nature photographers often stake out the Tower Falls area near Junction Butte, and the cliffs known as McMinn Bench between Mammoth and Gardiner, west of the 7,841-foot Mt. Everts. In spring, look for sheep perched on ledges above the highway. Ewes frequently congregate there to lamb before leading their brood in a westward migration to the backcountry around Electric Peak.

The MOUNTAIN GOAT
Climbing Colonizer

From any vantage point within Yellowstone, mountains are visible on the horizon. The park would therefore seem an excellent place to find billies and nannies, which occupy other high-elevation wildlands such as Glacier National Park. In fact, though, mountain goats (*Oreamnos americanus*) are only occasionally seen in the high peaks of the park's northwest and northeast corners.

According to fossil remains found at Palisades Reservoir in Idaho and at Pleistocene sites south and east of Yellowstone, goats may have lived near the park about 10,000 years ago, but then dispersed. For hunting purposes, these light-hooved alpinists were transplanted to areas near the park a number of years ago. Some descendants of those transplants have begun migrating into Yellowstone–a migration that the National Park Service regards as "artificial."

"During the past 30 years, one to fifteen goats have been reported at least seventeen times in the park, and on five occasions near the park. Of the seventeen in-park observations, six were in the northwest corner and eleven were in the northeast corner of the park," wrote research interpreter Norm Bishop in 1990.

The mountain goats are squarish and sure-footed, with long, yellowish-white fur and black, spiked horns. Males stand about 3 1/2 feet high and weigh between 120 and 250 pounds, while the females, which also have horns, are slightly smaller. Check the difference between white mountain goats and pale, female bighorn sheep before you conclude that you have seen a goat.

Where to Find Mountain Goats

Seeing a goat from the highway is a rare event. The northeast corner of the park, on the cliffs emanating from Baronnette Peak (north of the highway) and Abiather Peak (south of the highway), provides the best opportunity.

If you see a goat, write down the location and report it to a park ranger. In recent years, natural colonization (migration consistent with historical movement) of the park by mountain goats has occurred in the rocky canyons along U.S. Highway 191 (the far northwest corner of Yellowstone). Those goats will be allowed to repopulate the park because the colonization is considered consistent with the natural expansion of game territories as defined by the National Park Service's "natural regulation" policy.

The "artificial" population of goats invading Yellowstone from the northeast, however, may be prevented from establishing a niche here if it poses a threat to native vegetation and habitat important to the bighorn sheep.

BIRDS

The BALD EAGLE
Noble Presence in the Sky

On June 20, 1782, Congress declared the bald eagle a national wildlife symbol by placing its image on the Great Seal of the United States. Over the objection of Benjamin Franklin–who preferred the wild turkey–the eagle became an anthropomorphic trademark, first symbolizing liberty and rugged individualism, then in modern times becoming the emblem of a pristine and healthy environment.

Bald eagles (*Haliaeetus leucocephalus*) add another dimension to wildlife watching in Yellowstone, reminding all park visitors that the boundaries of a living, thriving ecosystem do not stop on the ground. The eagles force us to look skyward, and to understand that the noble goals of habitat protection extend to the clouds, where eagles and other species soar.

There are two species of eagle in Yellowstone, the easily recognizable bald and the golden eagle (*Aquila chrysaetos*), both of which are diurnal (day foraging) birds of prey. Eagles are also raptors and carnivores, meaning they aggressively seek out a protein-rich diet of fish, waterfowl, rodents, and small mammals, and scavenge from the carcasses of megafauna such as deer and elk. In other words, they hunt for meat.

Despite their smooth, hairless appearance, bald eagles are not really bald. Their name is derived from the Greek word *leucocephalus*, meaning "white-headed." The distinctive crown and tail feathers of a bald eagle take on their snowy-white tint only as a bird reaches adulthood. That process may take four or five years and involve five different molts (feather sheddings) before the bird assumes its famous profile. In the meantime, those unfamiliar with markings are prone to confuse immature bald eagles with golden eagles, because both are adorned with brown feathers.

Complementing their white markings, balds are highlighted by their yellow eyes and a prominent, arched yellow beak. While males and females have similar plumage, the females are usually larger. Adult balds of either sex, however, can develop wingspans reaching six to seven feet, giving them an imposing presence when compared to other birds in the park.

Eagles attract attention by virtue of their physical outline rather than their calls, which are not heard very often. If you study the plumage of their underside from the ground, you'll notice a darker band near the front of the wings and a fanned, pure white tail.

When not flying, bald eagles seek a clear vantage, often in the tallest of pine and cottonwood trees, from which to scout their surroundings. In a sitting posture, they are 2 1/2 to 3 feet tall.

It's natural to assume that Yellowstone–the world's first national park–is an idyllic setting for eagles, given its peerless surroundings and isolated location. Yet the park's chief ornithologist places the number of adult nesting pairs at about 15, and estimates that no more than 30 individuals winter here. Yellowstone's high-altitude topography is, at best, marginal for reproduction. Strong, blustery winds and notoriously inclement weather in the spring make nesting in Yellowstone difficult, and mortality among eaglets is high.

Bald eagles reside only on this continent, yet this national symbol was

reduced to staggeringly low numbers in the lower 48 states as late as the 1960s. Today balds are listed in 43 states as a federally endangered species under the provisions of the Endangered Species Act, the toughest wildlife protection law in the world.

Happily, bald eagles appear to be recovering, following further disastrous declines related to use of the pesticide DDT. The balds in Yellowstone are part of an overall "Greater Yellowstone" population that encompasses 14 million acres of contiguous lands, including two national parks, seven national forests, and three national wildlife refuges. The area is home to the largest nesting population of bald eagles in the western Rocky Mountains.

The Yellowstone area's most important role for bald eagles may be its use as a seasonal feeding area for migratory birds passing through in the spring and autumn. Several hundred eagles make a temporary stopover along the trout-rich environs of Yellowstone Lake and along the Yellowstone and Madison rivers on their way to wintering areas in the Pacific Northwest or the central Rockies of Colorado.

Where to Find Bald Eagles

Visit the shores of Yellowstone Lake, and look for bald eagles along the banks of the Yellowstone, Madison, and Snaker rivers south of Yellowstone in Grand Teton National Park.

As cutthroat trout start spawning in the Yellowstone River during early summer, the stretch of highway from Fishing Bridge to Hayden Valley may be a productive place to start your search.

During winter, when the majority of lakes and rivers freeze over, the hardy balds that stay behind cluster in trees at the edge of thermal features whose steam creates patches of open water. Occasionally, you may see eagles around such geothermal phenomena at West Thumb; at the confluence of the Madison and Firehole rivers; along the northern shores of Yellowstone Lake near Mary Bay; and on the Yellowstone River just north of Gardiner, along U.S. Highway 89.

The GOLDEN EAGLE
Hail the Mighty Soarer

Golden eagles, named for their brilliant crowns and lustrous brown plumage, are slightly smaller in stature than their cousins, the bald eagles. Yet, as champions of the wind, they soar like dominant giants, achieving primacy over the moody skies of Yellowstone.

Compared to all other birds of prey except balds, golden eagles (*Aquila chrysaetos*) are enormous, with wingspans measuring between five and seven feet and powerful talons for use in snatching live victims.

While areas where golden and bald eagles hunt may overlap in some park locations, the birds generally claim separate niches. Unlike balds, which rely on fish and carrion leftovers for primary nutrition, golden eagles fit the true predator mode, launching aerial dives with wings partially tucked as they pursue rodents and small mammals. Gifted with excellent eyesight, goldens can detect the slightest ground movement while circling in the sky. Their strength enables them to makes effortless turns in the breeze, propelled by leisurely flaps of their wings. Some intrepid dives take goldens to speeds of 160 miles per hour. When identifying golden eagles, look first to the color of the feathers, then to the head. From the ground, the outline of a golden resembles that of a hawk. A patch of white is visible on the fanned, grayish tailfeathers and between the brown and gray of the wings. It may take four years and two or three moltings (feather sheddings) until the adult bird's full feather coloration appears.

The crown of a golden eagle is, of course, golden, while its eyes are amber like the bald eagle's. The beak, though, is tipped with gray. The stare of a golden seems even more intense than a bald eagle's, because of dark shadowing in the eye sockets. Note, too, that brownish feathers cover the golden's legs clear to its talons.

Despite a reputation to the contrary, golden eagles rarely prey upon domestic livestock. Cases have been documented, though, and these attacks convinced ranchers earlier in this century to try to destroy the eagles. Today the practice is illegal, punishable by substantial fines under the Federal Eagle Act, which protects these amazing birds of prey.

Where to Find Golden Eagles

Though uncommon in Yellowstone, golden eagles can be seen in the early summer, drifting aloft over Lamar Valley near the confluence of the Lamar River and Soda Butte Creek. Goldens have also been known to prey on ducks in this area during the winter. The transitional landscape here makes ideal habitat for eagles. It combines flat, grassy terrain with undulating foothills to provide eagles with a diversity of available food.

The OSPREY
Fearless Divebomber

Yellowstone's least-known daredevil is the osprey (*Pandion haliaetus*). Within the Grand Canyon of the Yellowstone and along the shores of Yellowstone Lake, this eagle-like raptor finds solitude among rock and pine fortresses beyond the reach of human intrusion.

The same species of osprey present in Yellowstone occurs around the world, recognized by some admirers as the "fish hawk." However, in few other corners of the globe do the behavioral acrobatics seem so splendid. Although males and females often strike a courtship that lasts for years, males swoon their mate through an impressive display–vaulting abruptly into the sky and falling downward again.

The bushel-like nests of osprey are visible in the Grand Canyon at the top of rhyolite (volcanic rock) pillars. Constructed of large twigs, the nests are amazingly durable in the park's strong winds. Some 20 miles south of the canyon, osprey are common over the airy expanses of Yellowstone Lake, home to many of the park's sixty nesting pairs.

When spotting osprey, follow the white headfeathers under the neck to the white breast, which give way to marbled brown-and-white feathers under the wings and a striped pattern that stretches across the fan-like tail.

Where to Find Osprey

Osprey range most frequently in the Grand Canyon of the Yellowstone, over Yellowstone Lake, and along the Yellowstone River.

The RED-TAILED HAWK
Rodent-Rich Raptor

When forest fires swept through Yellowstone in 1988, a canopy of darkness was lifted from some 790,000 acres, or more than one-third of the park. A sprawling blanket of over-mature conifers, labeled by some botanists as "a lodgepole pine desert," was abrubtly recycled. Fertilized by nutrient-rich ash, the forest floor began erupting–as it is today–with plant life that will continue to burgeon for the next half-century.

One species likely to benefit from the fresh glint of sunshine in burned areas is the red-tailed hawk. As plants rapidly regrow, a thriving community of vegetarian rodents is emerging, and these rodents are the prime food source of hawks, owls, and other birds of prey.

Red-tails (*Buteo jamaicensis*) are the first raptors that visitors may encounter from the roadside. Whether soaring above an open meadow or perched in a strategic treetop, red-tails in the park go about their business with little fear of humans. The skittishness found in other members of the hawk family is absent in red-tails, which have adjusted well to human development across North America.

More research is needed on red-tails, but park scientists say the number of birds is related to the health of its prey species, which include a variety of mammals and reptiles from rabbits and mice to snakes and squirrels. Widely dispersed across all of the lower 48 states, red-tails are easy to identify. They are also the most abundant species of hawk in the park.

While flying above, red-tails reveal a classic hawk profile, with wings that extend more than three feet across and a fanned tail. The coloration is distinct. There are brown feathers on the head and rimming the outside tips of the wings. In a sitting position, the red-brown tail is visible, as are the dark brown plumage and the yellowish feet.

Where To Find Red-tailed Hawks

Visit the sagebrush meadows near Roosevelt-Tower Junction and the open, rolling grasslands around the McMinn Bench and the northern park entrance. Red-tails are also spotted frequently between the Swan Lake flats and Norris Junction, and in the Lamar Valley.

The PEREGRINE FALCON
Bird on the Comeback Trail

The peregrine falcon's plight reminds us all how fragile the web of life can be. An efficient and ferocious predator, the peregrine (*Falco peregrinus*) can tear through the air like a bullet to catch its principal prey, a duck or songbird. Not so long ago, ingestion of that same prey often proved lethal.

With the use of DDT rampant in the United States until the pesticide was banned in 1972, birds of prey representing dozens of species were tragically wiped out. While the pesticide was toxic to insects and small mammals, the effect on raptors like peregrines was more insidious. The chemical entered the birds' bodies through secondary ingestion. Eggs from female raptors became so brittle or thin-shelled that young could not develop. The falcon population was among those that plummeted.

According to federal biologists, the peregrine was on the verge of extinction east of the Mississippi by 1960, and ten years later the same fate awaited those birds within the Yellowstone ecosystem. The grim statistics prompted calls for the peregrine to be listed as a federally endangered species in 1969. Through support from the federal government and the non-profit Peregrine Fund, based in Boise, Idaho, peregrine falcons are now quickly reclaiming their old niche in and around Yellowstone. Over 500 birds were hacked (released) in the Greater Yellowstone area between 1980 and 1991, and at least 75 breeding pairs were established in the wild.

Yellowstone contains excellent falcon terrain, and peregrines are regularly sighted within the park. Still, only remote and rocky sections of the park are desirable for these cliff-dwelling avians. About 14 peregrines inhabit Yellowstone itself, and the likelihood that the number will increase depends on construction of successful eyries (nests) and production of young birds that fledge.

Peregrines can be identified by their intense features–black feathers that resemble a helmet, pointed "falcon" wings and tail, and a light gray chest streaked with dark gray markings. When the bird is sitting, fuller dark-gray feathers are visible on its back. Despite its potency as a predator, the peregrine is relatively small, attaining an average adult wingspan of just over three feet. Falconers admire the peregrine for its ability to hunt and to reach speeds of 200 miles per hour.

The outlook for peregrines in the national park is favorable, but don't expect to see them often from the roadside. While they have become popular fixtures of the skyline in many urban areas, here they are creatures that thrive on seclusion.

Where to Find Peregrine Falcons

Scan the cliffs in the northeast corner of the park and in Hayden Valley, particularly along the western side of the highway.

The GREAT GRAY OWL
Spooky Hooter

There may be nothing spookier than staring at a pile of fallen timber and noticing that the two yellow eyes of an owl are staring back.

When we venture into great gray owl habitat, a certain mandate comes with the territory–a mandate to stay alert, lest you miss some incredible wildlife watching. Great gray owls (*Strix nebulosa*) are diurnal, haunting the forested clearings day and night, which makes them accessible for viewing. In Yellowstone, where these raptors are probably more common than they seem, the majority of owl sightings occur at dusk and dawn. The great gray has a classic owl shape–an elliptical face, protruding concentric patterns around the eyes, and a puffed and feathery frame. Its feathers, of course, are gray, streaked with white and dark brown. When it calls, it emits the stereotypical "hoo, hoo" sound. Native American tribes have identified this owl as both a good omen that speaks truths and a bad omen that portends doom. During your visit to the park, you decide.

At home in middle-elevation coniferous forests, the great gray is one of the largest owls in North America, sporting a wingspan of nearly three feet. To ensure that there is plenty of wing clearance when it stalks prey, the great gray hunts on the edges of meadows.

Males and females look alike, and ornithologists say it's not unusual to find great grays foraging in pairs, which makes them easier to spot and identify. Nonetheless, sighting them along the highway is difficult. Best estimates suggest that fewer than 100 pairs nest in Yellowstone. Some of those migrate south during the coldest winter months, while others remain.

Where to Find Great Gray Owls

Look for great grays in meadows south of Canyon Village, and in the clearings that border burned patches of forest northwest of Roosevelt-Tower Junction. In recent years, a resident pair of great grays has been spotted in meadows about one mile west of Canyon Village on the road to Norris Junction.

The AMERICAN WHITE PELICAN
Gregarious Fisherbird

American white pelicans (*Pelecanus erythrorhynchos*) are gregarious creatures whose frequent flapping and squawking make them favorites among birders and avian photographers. Their penchant for assembling in groups makes them easy to identify from the roadside.

The pelican is endowed with a long, voluminous bill that helps it catch and shovel fish from the waterways it inhabits. As the name implies, the bird's feathery covering is white, though a gentle dusting of black covers the top of the head. As a pelican passes overhead, note the black primary and secondary feathers on the backs and tips of its wings. If you remain uncertain whether you've seen a pelican, look for the bird's long, orange-yellow bill and its orange, webbed feet.

During the trout spawn, you may see pelicans netting more than one fish at a time, holding them in a throat pouch known as the gular, then swallowing their catch whole.

White pelicans are common in Yellowstone Lake and along the outgoing portions of the Yellowstone River, but elsewhere in the western United States their numbers have plummeted due to habitat destruction and the long-term effects of the now-banned pesticide DDT. Because they are endemic to relatively small regions of the lower U.S., pelicans are considered extremely important. Park tourists eagerly form their own flocks near pelican feeding areas, but observation of pelicans should occur only from a distance, as the birds are easily disturbed.

Between 200 and 400 pairs of pelicans nest in Yellowstone during the summer months, but the number can fluctuate radically depending on water levels in Yellowstone Lake. When rain and melting spring snow suddenly flood the lakeshore, hundreds of pelican eggs can be lost, but when the weather is less inclement and predation by coyotes is low, the peak population of pelicans in the park may swell to as many as 1,000 birds.

Migratory flyers, pelicans return each spring to the park. Researchers suggest that the Great Salt Lake on the edge of Salt Lake City, Utah, serves as a staging ground for pelicans before their April arrival in Yellowstone. When the pelicans leave in late September, they again migrate to Salt Lake before embarking on a journey to winter havens along the coastlines of California and Mexico.

Human attraction to these delightful seasonal residents leaves them vulnerable to habitat disruption, so park officials have closed all nesting areas to the public. Approaching a nest can cause adult birds to abandon their eggs or their featherless young, which may mean that a crop of young pelicans will never have the opportunity to hatch or fledge. Fortunately, most of the pelican rookeries are located offshore, on islands of Yellowstone Lake that are inaccessible to coyotes and most people.

Where to Find American White Pelicans

Pelican Creek, a tributary of Yellowstone Lake, was so named because a pelican was shot by an explorer there in 1863. While birds are still seen at the mouth of the creek as it enters Yellowstone Lake, they're found more often on the northwestern shores of the lake from Mary Bay southward to Pumice Point in the West Thumb region. Look for pelicans along the Yellowstone River as well, especially from Fishing Bridge north to the wildlife overlooks in Hayden Valley.

The GREAT BLUE HERON
Knobby-Kneed Water Wader

Great blue herons (*Ardea herodias*) are the quintessential water waders, strolling on their long, pole-like legs through shallow pools or shores where minnows and aquatic vegetation are abundantly available.

Herons are far more common to North America than sandhill cranes, and Yellowstone straddles the edge of the heron's range in the Rockies. Adult herons stand almost four feet tall, about 25 percent taller than adult sandhills.

The most efficient way to distinguish between herons and cranes is to focus on shape. The more robust herons are stork-like in appearance, maintaining an S-shaped neck while either standing or flying. The heron sports a long, golden bill, and a stringy plumb of feathers extending from its neck over the breast area. As the name connotes, the great blue's feathers are bluish-gray, highlighted by black patches on the shoulders, abdomen, and the top of the head. White-tinted feathers are also present beneath the bird's yellow eyes, along the front curve of its neck, and down the middle of the abdomen. Males and females are generally similar in appearance.

Raids by coyotes on nest sites and human intrusions are the leading causes of mortality among heron fledglings. People who are caught disturbing the birds can be issued a citation and fine, so observe these fascinating creatures from a distance.

Where to Find Great Blue Herons

Look for herons along the Madison River, particularly in the area around Seven Mile Bridge, and near Fishing Bridge on the northern shore of Yellowstone Lake. Beyond the park boundary in eastern Idaho, the upper stretches of the Snake River form a valuable natural rookery for herons in the Greater Yellowstone ecosystem.

The SANDHILL CRANE
Long-Distance Migrator

Sandhill cranes (*Grus canadensis*), like great blue herons, are masters of subtlety. The size and apparently awkward construction of these gangling birds might lead you to believe that they lack the coordination necessary to endure the rugged sub-alpine environment of Yellowstone. But their appearance is merely a brilliant disguise.

Lifting slowly from the rivers, lakes, and meadows of the park, sandhills appear to painstakingly pull themselves from their terrestrial vantages, rising tentatively into the wind. Once airborne, however, they accelerate into effortless, balletic glides. Similarities in shape frequently cause wildlife watchers to mistake sandhills for great blues, but upon closer examination they are distinctly different.

While sandhills and great blues are occasionally found in the same habitat, they usually thrive in different ecological niches. Sandhills, though classified as waterfowl, often prefer to plant their knobby-kneed legs on dry, solid ground. Herons, on the other hand, gravitate to calm and tranquil water surfaces free of swift currents and heavy breezes. The calls of cranes and herons also differ. Cranes emit a sonorous "kroo-oooo" and "garooo-ahh," while herons issue boisterous and curt "graaak."

The adult sandhill, which stands three to four feet tall, is predominantly gray, with a willowy frame and a long, narrow neck held slightly bent. A crane's head is adorned by a patch of red over the eyes and forehead, with a dark bill far smaller than a heron's. The body plumage of some adult birds may assume a reddish hue, due to the iron oxide soil transferred onto feathers when the birds preen.

In flight the crane's body is fully extended, from its bill to the end of its non-webbed feet. Sandhills are similar in appearance, though smaller, to their rare cousin, the whooping cranes. In fact, sandhills have been used to roost as surrogate parents over whooping crane eggs, in an attempt to restore a natural population of whoopers to the wild.

Female sandhills (which are identical in appearance to males) will build their nests in meadows temporarily submerged by spring rain and melting snow, a task usually accomplished by early May. If the nests are not disturbed by humans or preying coyotes, as many as three eggs may hatch, producing young that fledge in late summer and join adult birds in leaving Yellowstone by mid-autumn.

Although there is a breeding population of sandhills in Yellowstone, it's uncertain how many of the birds inhabiting wetlands along the roadside are transient. During the summer, sandhill visitors fly back and forth from sanctuaries well beyond the park's periphery. Federal ornithologists say that 200 cranes may inhabit the park at the peak of seasonal occupation, yet only about 60 pairs annually nest here.

The sandhills you see in Yellowstone are long-distance travelers, spending the cold winter months along the Rio Grande River in southern New Mexico, or across the border in Mexico. Each April they gather in V-shaped flocks and fly all the way back to the northern Rockies.

Where to Find Sandhill Cranes

Cranes often walk on land–though usually in close proximity to water–perusing meadows for insects, small rodents, seeds, and roots. One spot where this routine can be seen from the roadside is off of Fountain Flats Drive in the Lower Geyser Basin–a secondary road open seasonally to motorists. Another good area is along the Swan Lake flats south of Mammoth Hot Springs. Adult sandhills gather food from these locations and carry it back to hatchlings waiting in nests miles away. Also look for sandhills near Obsidian Creek and in Hayden Valley.

The TRUMPETER SWAN
Nature's Jumbo Jet

The sight of a trumpeter swan (*Cygnus buccinator*) grazing the misty surface of a pond while in wing-locked flight is a regal and inspiring one. This species of swan, native only to North America, commonly leaves both poets and wildlife watchers smitten.

The trumpeter serves as a powerful metaphor for wildlife conservation in the 20th century. Once headed toward extinction south of Canada, the trumpeter has managed its most successful comeback within the Yellowstone ecosystem. A visit to either Yellowstone or Grand Teton national parks can offer a rare glimpse of these snow-white marvels, which might be considered the jumbo jets of the bird world.

Trumpeters are the largest waterfowl in the world, and easily the biggest flyers in Yellowstone. The wingspan of males (cobs) can reach seven feet, and though females (pens) are smaller, their beauty is no less profound. Cobs weigh between 25 and 30 pounds, while pens weigh between 23 and 27 pounds. The trumpeter is generally bigger and heavier than an eagle.

Most wildlife watchers, though, will recognize trumpeters by their sensuous form. They are long-necked and entirely white except for their black bills and webbed feet. Unlike their domesticated cousin, the mute swan, trumpeters swim with their necks held straight in a distinguished manner. Despite their sometimes frail appearance, trumpeters are hardy, enduring temperatures that reach 40 to 50 degrees below zero in winter. Native Americans and early European explorers identified the approach of trumpeters by their distinctive "koh-hoh, koh-hoh" calls.

It's a marvel that these endemic swans have managed to survive. By the middle of the 19th century, market hunters had almost exterminated trumpeters from coast to coast. Ironically, the trumpeter's marvelous plumage led to its near-demise, as feathers were taken from slaughtered birds and used to adorn high-fashion hats. Many feared the trumpeter would disappear forever.

Miraculously, a small population was counted in isolated waters of Yellowstone early in the 20th century. During the 1930s, fewer than 50 were identified by federal biologists, all that remained of the tens of thousands that once graced the skies and the countryside. An alarm was sounded in the halls of Congress, and the Red Rock Lakes National Wildlife Refuge west of Yellowstone was set aside to facilitate trumpeter recovery efforts.

Yellowstone's resident swan population has undergone population swings, because inclement weather and predation by coyotes takes a serious toll on the production of young swans, called cygnets. About 30 resident trumpeters currently inhabit Yellowstone, though the number has ranged from a peak of 49 adults in recent years to fewer than 25. Less than 15 nesting pairs of swans reside in the park, an ever-decreasing number that concerns ornithologists.

In recent years, the National Park Service has taken measures to reduce trumpeter mortality, including a program to ban lead fishing sinkers (which

may injure birds), making sure there are no power lines located near watersheds, and reducing human impact on nest sites. Visitors have an integral role to play in protecting swans for future generations. Please observe trumpeters from a distance, and never approach nesting birds. Any disruption to nest sites can have severe consequences for the local swan population.

Where to Find Trumpeter Swans

The best habitat for swans in the region is not found in Yellowstone, but on lowland waters west of the park that remain open during the harshest winter conditions. However, each autumn, wildlife watchers see hundreds of trumpeters that find temporary shelter in Yellowstone before most of the park's waters freeze over. Toward December, these migrants move on to winter feeding areas in eastern Idaho and southwest Montana.

Specifically, you may find swans near the Seven Mile Bridge on the Madison River; on the appropriately named Swan Lake south of Mammoth Hot Springs; and along the Yellowstone River between Fishing Bridge and Hayden Valley.

During the winter, snowmobilers and cross-country skiers can see trumpeters on stretches of open water along the Yellowstone and Madison rivers, where tepid water from geothermal features prevents areas from freezing over.

The CANADA GOOSE
Hardy Honker

Most park visitors know that it's not proper etiquette to honk their car horns in approval of Yellowstone's wildlife. Not only can the sound disrupt and frighten animals, it also spoils the essence of the park as a retreat away from the cacophony of urban living. Besides, there's one resident of Yellowstone that provides all the honking a homesick urbanite will ever need–the Canada goose.

For eons, perhaps, Canada geese (*Branta canadensis*), also known as Canada honkers, have sounded their way across the flyways of North America. Passing overhead in V-shaped squadrons, these hardy members of the duck family are abundant in most sub-alpine areas of Yellowstone.

The goose's coloration is precise. Its oblong black neck is tipped by a black beak, but flared by a half-ring of white running from beneath the eyes down under the throat. From the bottom of the neck, the wide body is grayish-brown, with a black tail. The bird's underside has whitish feathers on the belly and tail.

Every so often a goose is surprised by a coyote, but such predation is rare because geese are gregarious, alert, and fly if spooked. Adults stand about three feet tall, and weigh between 8 and 12 pounds.

Although the park does host a year-round population of Canadas, many that you see are transient, coming from Canadian prairies in September and October or from the Gulf of Mexico in April and May. The bird's classic "uh-honnnk" is audible as flocks pass over at low elevations.

Where to Find Canada Geese

Canadas are common in Hayden Valley along the grassy banks of the Yellowstone River, where they feed on green stems and aquatic plants. You'll also find them in the Lower Geyser Basin along the Firehole River, north of Norris Junction along the Gibbon River, and in Lamar Valley along the Lamar River.

A YELLOWSTONE GALLERY

Porcupine
Erethizon dorsatum

The prickly pear of the mammal world, the porcupine carries some 30,000 quills in its quiver, and each barbed quill can deliver a stinging reminder that the animal prefers to be left alone. However, contrary to myth, a porcupine can't "shoot" its quills at intruders. The surest signs of porcupine presence are their tracks–the front paws indicate four toes with claws, while the back paws reveal five claws–and the "cat faces" the animal creates when it chews away the bark of trees. Porcupines are widely dispersed in the forests of Yellowstone, and are common along stretches of highway that dissect stands of old growth timber. Look in the early morning or late evening.

Snowshoe Hare
Lepus americanus

"A jackrabbit wearing snowshoes." That's how one park ranger describes the snowshoe hare. It thrives in the wooded, alpine environment of Yellowstone, where snowfall is often measured in feet rather than inches. Graced with extraordinarily wide paws, the snowshoe leaves large hind prints in snow. The impressions also show the snowshoe's toes, which are spread wide apart. The snowshoe camouflages itself by taking on a cloak of white fur from October through March, then turns a brownish color in spring. Though ubiquitous in the park, it's seldom seen in daylight. Look for snowshoes in the Canyon and Lake areas, and in the park's northeast corner.

Beaver
Castor canadensis

The very symbol of industriousness, the dam-building beaver has the power to shape the future of streams in Yellowstone and adjacent habitat. Known as a busy logger with curved, buck teeth, the beaver can also be identified by its webbed hind feet, lush brown coat, and paddle-like tail. Beaver presence is indicated by dams, domed lodges partially immersed in water, and tree stumps gnawed to a conical point. You'll find them hard at work just before dusk and dawn. The Yellowstone, Gardiner, and Lamar rivers in the northern third of the park are good places to start your search. In recent years, beavers have colonized the creeks that straddle U.S. Highway 191 in the park's northwest corner.

In a shallow pond setting, the muskrat's house–constructed of cattails, reeds, mud, and twigs–resembles a miniature beaver lodge. In deep lakes or fast-flowing streams, it digs burrows with underwater entrances in shorelines and banks. A muskrat's tail is long, flattened, and leathery. Its hind feet are webbed, but the front paws are equipped with claws used for gripping the plants, crayfish, and fish that make up its diet. Muskrats remain active in winter, and you're most likely to see them at dusk or dawn. The swimming mammals inhabit the same areas populated by beavers. You can view them in the ponds of Lamar River Valley, Beaver Ponds, and Obsidian Creek, or along the Snake and Madison rivers.

Muskrat
Ondatra zibethicus

The largest member of the weasel family is the "street fighter" of the forest. It will confront mountain lions or bears in order to protect its share of a carcass. The wolverine's brawny frame is built low to the ground, and it can weigh as much as 50 pounds. Sometimes wildlife watchers mistake it for a bear. Look for patches of light, grayish hair on the flat top of the wolverine's head, and a brown or yellowish streak down the back that extends nearly to the rump. So scarce are they in Yellowstone that any sighting is immediately investigated by park rangers. Sightings have been reported in recent years in the northeast corner of the park, between Pebble Creek campground and the northeast entrance.

Wolverine
Gulo luscus

Weasels are great fun to watch. They're skinny chameleons, capable of changing the color of their coats to match the landscape. Pound for pound, they're among nature's most formidable predators, weighing eight ounces or less but preying on animals twice their size. Brown with light tan belly fur during the summer, the weasel begins molting late in the season, replacing its brown fur with a coat of white hair that serves as winter camouflage. You'll find the long-tailed variety along most of the rivers and lakes in Yellowstone, and the ermine (short-tailed) is viewable from most wooded trails in the park. It often occupies wetlands at elevations of 5,000 to 9,000 feet.

Short and **Long-tailed Weasel**
Mustela erminea/Mustela frenata

Pine Marten
Martes americana

The pine marten resembles a weasel, but it's larger and brownish in color, with a tail that constitutes a third of its two-foot body length. The marten is a tree-dwelling resident of old-growth forests, finding shelter under dark, coniferous canopies. To assess its size, think of it as bigger than a mink but smaller than a fisher. Pine martens are rare in the park, though they have been seen near Pebble Creek campground in the northeast corner, Canyon Village, the Lake development, and on the western shore of Yellowstone Lake. In winter, they're spotted near Snow Lodge at Old Faithful.

Mink
Mustela vison

Where muskrats are present, mink are not far away, because the famous fur bearers enjoy eating their vegetarian neighbors. Larger than the weasel and slightly smaller than the pine marten, mink measure up to 2 1/2 feet, with long tails and chocolate or reddish brown fur prized by trappers. The mink is a capable swimmer, and its ability to flee on either land or water makes it less vulnerable to predators. Look for mink wherever you find muskrats, in most of the park's riverways, and in ponds where rats are present. During the winter, mink are seen along the Yellowstone and Lamar rivers, running across the ice.

Fisher
Martes martes

The fisher has all the classic trademarks of a mustelid–a long, tubular body, a bushy tail, and short legs. In fact, a fisher looks like an oversized mink. Adults can reach weights of 12 to 18 pounds and lengths of over three feet. Part climber, part swimmer, and part burrower, the fisher lives in untamed backcountry, and is the rarest of the nine members of the weasel family found in Yellowstone. The park lies at the southernmost tip of the fisher's range, and you're not likely to spot one from the highway.

A badger's entire life is centered around digging dirt–whether making its dens, escaping from enemies, or finding gophers on which to snack. The badger has a low, tank-like frame, with muscular forearms and curved claws. A vivid white line of fur runs the length of its snout, across its flattened head, and along portions of the upper backbone. Patches of white between the eyes and the ears are ornamented by hooks of black. A marbled pattern of gray and brown covers the rest of its back and rump, providing camouflage. You'll find badgers in the sagebrush meadows of the park, specifically in the Tower-Roosevelt area, in Lamar Valley, and around Mammoth Hot Springs. The animal is fiercely territorial and does not hesitate to charge intruders.

Badger
Taxidea tuxus

An oblong creature fond of blissfully spinning, tumbling, and swishing in the currents, the river otter is a joy to watch. Yellowstone, which does not allow boat or canoe traffic on its rivers, is one of the few spots in the northern Rockies where development does not threaten otter habitat. Otters are the largest of the marine mustelids, and their long, narrow frames are typical of members of the weasel family. They are three to four feet long, with long tails, webbed feet, grayish whiskers, and brownish bellies that are lighter than the remainder of their fur. You'll find them throughout the Yellowstone River drainage, along calm stretches of the river from Otter Creek to Fishing Bridge, and near the picnic area in Lamar Valley.

River Otter
Lutra canadensis

Yellowstone visitors will probably hear pikas before they actually see the animal. Labeled "whistling hares," pikas are hare-shaped but in fact resemble pet shop guinea pigs. The pika has reddish-brown fur; wide, rounded ears; white paws; and no tail. It sounds a shrill, high-pitched bleat (or whistle) whenever it's threatened. In the park, the pika's bleat is often noted not only by humans but by hungry weasels or birds of prey. You'll find pikas at "the Hoodoos" between Mammoth and Golden Gate, and in the rocks along the Madison River not far from Seven Mile Bridge.

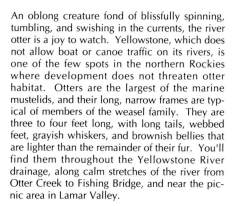

Pika
Ochotona princeps

Yellow-bellied Marmot
Marmota flaviventrus

Marmots and pikas share a similar ecological niche, haunting the park's higher elevations. The yellow-bellied marmot is also known as "the whistle pig," because it emits a screeching call when threatened by predators. Marmots are frumpy, resembling fat squirrels, but they're surprisingly mobile. As the name suggests, they have fluffy, yellowish fur on their underbellies. Their backs are covered with gray-tinted hair that also has yellow underneath. Marmots are common along high-altitude sections of the highway, including Craig Pass, Sylvan Pass, Dunraven Pass, and near Canyon Village.

Least Chipmunk
Tamias minimus

You might encounter a least chipmunk playing a deadly game of hide and seek with its mortal enemy, the weasel. The least is often found in coniferous forests where fallen logs or rock piles are present. Although it doesn't hibernate in the more southerly regions of the Rockies, the tiny animal is driven into winter slumber here by the bitter cold. Like all chipmunks, the least has black and white stripes running across its face and down its back, but has orange side fur that is less pronounced than other species. It sports a short, fluffed, grayish-brown tail. Like its larger cousin, the yellow-pine, the least chipmunk can be spotted at Sheepeater Cliff and at campgrounds throughout the park.

Uinta Ground Squirrel
Spermophilus armatus

This reddish-gray member of the squirrel family shows no squeamishness around humans, and knows how to entertain a crowd with its high-energy antics. Avoid offering it food, though, because animal feeding has no place in the park, and because you might get bitten. The Uinta appears to be a cross between two other Yellowstone inhabitants–the red squirrel and the yellow-bellied marmot. It's generally larger than the red squirrel and smaller than the marmot. The Uinta inhabits only a small section of the northern Rockies, and it spends seven months of the year in hibernation. You'll find it along the boardwalks of Old Faithful, near Canyon Village, on the old army parade grounds at Mammoth, and in the sagebrush meadows east of Roosevelt Lodge.

A main attraction for nature lovers at the park's Le Hardy Rapids is a small, clown-like duck known as the harlequin. The colorful bird is one of the rarest species of waterfowl in the Rockies, and is rivaled in coloration only by the drake wood duck. The male harlequin's vivid blend of white, slate blue, and chestnut plumage resembles the facial make-up of a circus clown. These migratory birds have a low tolerance for human intrusion, and their numbers have declined steadily. As a result, Le Hardy Rapids will be subject to temporary closures from April until early June for several years, to allow harlequins to breed and lay eggs without human disruption. Harlequins can be spotted there at other times, and are visible in summer from the Tower Falls Trail along the Yellowstone River.

Harlequin Duck
Histrionicus histrionicus

Blue and ruffed grouse occupy different types of forest. Blues prefer high ridgelines in coniferous forests, where they feast on pine needles and grasshoppers. The ruffed grouse sticks to the lower deciduous forests of aspen, willow, and cottonwood. Blues are large by grouse standards, with long necks, bluish-gray feathers on their backs and necks, and a slit of yellow near the eyes. Ruffed grouse are more brownish, with buffed feather patches and brown and white-streaked bellies. The ruffed engage in a wing-beating mating ritual called "drumming." You'll find blue grouse near the northeastern shore of Yellowstone Lake, and over Craig, Sylvan, and Dunraven passes. Ruffed grouse are often spotted in aspen groves northwest of the Roosevelt-Tower Junction and near Mammoth.

Blue and **Ruffed Grouse**
Dendragapus obscurus
Bonasa umbellus

Talkative and irreverent, ravens respond to disruptions (such as hikers) with a screaming "krrrraaaak-kraa." Members of the crow family, they pervade all developed areas of Yellowstone, playing a dual role as beggars and predators. More than 2 1/2 feet tall, the raven is crow-like, but its frame and beak are larger than the crow's and its plumage is radiant black. Scruffy feathers may be visible in the throat area. Ravens may terrorize song-birds by raiding their nests and "ravenously" consuming the eggs or young birds. You'll find these gregarious carrion-eaters near picnic areas and campsites, at all eleven park developments, and wherever carcasses are present. In fact, they may lead you to other animals.

Common Raven
Corvus corvax

So You'd Like to Know More?

Here's a list of further educational opportunities for wildlife watchers.

Yellowstone Association. Founded in 1933, the Yellowstone Association is committed to assisting the public in all matters of natural history education. From membership fees and sales of books at visitor centers, the Association raises funds that are directed toward better interpretation of wildlife, geologic resources, and cultural sites. For a membership in the Association or for more information, write: Yellowstone Association, P.O. Box 117, Yellowstone National Park, WY 82190.

Yellowstone Institute. For wildlife watchers interested in learning about specific animals in the park, the non-profit Yellowstone Institute offers a variety of courses, including some that can be used to accrue academic credit. Located at the old Buffalo Ranch in Lamar Valley, the Institute presents both resident and day programs for modest fees. To obtain a copy of the Institute's course catalog, write Yellowstone Institute, P.O. Box 117, Yellowstone National Park, WY 82190.

Teton Science School. Based at the edge of Grand Teton National Park in scenic Jackson Hole, the Teton Science School offers courses that explore subjects including wildlife watching in the Yellowstone ecosystem. For more information, write Teton Science School, P.O. Box 68-B, Kelly, WY 83011

Self-Guided Nature Trails. Visitors who would like a glimpse of the Yellowstone backcountry without having to walk long distances should consider the nature trails that are interspersed throughout the park. Wildlife can be seen from these trails, and they provide a great opportunity for exercise. Nature trails are located at Tower Falls, Mud Volcano, Norris Geyser Basin, the Upper Geyser Basin at Old Faithful, the Firehole Lake Drive, Fountain Paint Pots, Grand Canyon of the Yellowstone, and Mammoth Hot Springs.

Bibliography

In terms of its wildlife, plants and geothermal features, Yellowstone is one of the most studied parks on the planet. Amassing an impressive library of data, the park research office was a helpful resource in compiling information for this book. Much of the information was gleaned from previous discussions with park researchers in the form of personal interviews or assignments for newspaper and magazine articles. What follows is a summary of my sources.

Barbee, Robert, Yellowstone Superintendent, numerous interviews between 1987 and 1991.

Bishop, Norman, Population Status of Large Mammals in Yellowstone National Park. June 12, 1990.

Bishop, Norman, Yellowstone's research interpreter, numerous personal communications between 1987 and 1991.

Brown, Gary, Yellowstone's former assistant chief ranger and head of grizzly bear management in the park. Numerous personal communications between 1987 and 1991.

Clark, Tim, Ann H. Harvey, Robert D. Dom, David L. Genter, and Craig Groves. Rare, Sensitive, and Threatened Species of the Greater Yellowstone Ecosystem prepared by the Northern Rockies Conservation Cooperative, Montana Natural Heritage Program, The Nature Conservancy–Idaho, Montana, and Wyoming Field Offices and Mountain West Environmental Services 1989.

Coleman, Stu. Yellowstone resource specialist, numerous personal communications between 1989 and 1991.

Consolo, S.L. Beaver in Yellowstone National Park. Yellowstone Research Office. 1990.

Crabtree, Dr. Robert., Yellowstone coyote researcher, personal communication 1991.

Craighead, Karen. Large Mammals of Yellowstone and Grand Teton National Parks. 1978.

Despain, Don, Douglas Houston, Mary Meagher, Paul Schullery, *Wildlife in Transition; Man and Nature on Yellowstone's Northern Range.* Boulder: Roberts Rinehart 1986.

Despain, Don G., *Yellowstone Vegetation.* Boulder: Roberts Rinehart. 1990.

Frye, Steve, Yellowstone's assistant chief ranger, personal communications in 1991.

Glick, Dennis. An Environmental Profile of the Greater Yellowstone Ecosystem. Prepared for Greater Yellowstone Coalition, 1991.

Grazing Influences on Yellowstone's Northern Range, Research Summaries Compiled by Francis Singer July 15, 1989.

Grazing influences on Yellowstone's Northern Range, Research Summaries Compiled by Francis Singer August 15, 1990.

The Greater Yellowstone Area; an aggregation of National Park and National Forest Management Plans. 1987.

Greater Yellowstone Ecosystem; An analysis of data submitted by federal and state agencies prepared by the Congressional Research Service/Library of Congress, for Congress 1987.

Hadly, Elizabeth A. Holocene mammalian fauna of Lamar Cave, Yellowstone National Park and its implications for ecosystem dynamics. Prepared for Yellowstone Research Office and Department of Quaternary Studies, Northern Arizona University, 1989.

Haines, Aubrey. *The Yellowstone Story.* Boulder; Colorado Associated University Press. 1977.

Herrero, Stephen. *Bear Attacks; Their Causes and Avoidance.* New York: Nick Lyons Books. 1985.

Houston, Douglas B. *The Northern Yellowstone Elk.* New York: Macmillan Publishing Co., Inc. 1982.

Janetski, Joel C., *Indians of Yellowstone Park.* Salt Lake City: University of Utah Press 1987.

Koehler, G.M. and M.G. Hornocker. A preliminary survey of mountain lions in Yellowstone National Park. Report to Yellowstone. 1986.

Langford, Nathaniel Pitt. *The Discovery of Yellowstone Park.* Lincoln: University of Nebraska Press. 1972.

Laundre, Dr. John W. The status, distribution, and management of mountain goats in the Greater Yellowstone Ecosystem. Delivered to National Park Service, September 1990.

Matthiessen, Peter. *Wildlife in America.* New York: Viking Penguin. 1987.

McEneaney, Terry. *Birds of Yellowstone.* Boulder: Roberts Rinehart, Inc. Publishers 1989-1991.

McEneaney, Terry. Yellowstone ornithologist, personal communications 1989-1991.

Yellowstone Wildlife: A Watcher's Guide

Meagher, Mary. An Outbreak of Pinkeye in Bighorn Sheep, Yellowstone National Park, report delivered to Biennial Symposium of the North American Wild Sheep and Goat Conference. 1982.

Meagher, Mary. Cougar and Wolverine in Yellowstone National Park, Yellowstone Research Office, June 1986.

Meagher, Mary. "Yellowstone's Free-Ranging Bison." Article in Naturalist Magazine Volume 36, No. 3, 1985.

Meagher, Mary. Chapter called "Bison" for book, *Big Game of North America.* Stackpole Books. 1978.

Meagher, Mary. Yellowstone Bison. Prepared for Yellowstone Research Office. 1986.

Meagher, Mary. Bison researcher and scientist, personal communications 1990-1991

Mech, L. David, *The Wolf; The Ecology and Behavior of an Endangered Species.* Minneapolis: University of Minnesota Press 1970.

Miller Jr., Arthur P. *Park Ranger Guide to Wildlife.* Harrisburg: Stackpole Books 1990.

Miller, Millie, and Cyndi Nelson. *Talons: North American Birds of Prey.* Boulder: Johnson Books. 1989

Muir, John. *Our National Parks.* Foreword by Alfred Runte. San Francisco: Sierra Club Books. 1991.

Murie, Adolph, Ecology of the Coyote in the Yellowstone U.S. Government Printing Office 1940.

Murphy, Kerry M. and Jay W. Tischendorf. Ecology of the Mountain Lion in the Northern Yellowstone Ecosystem. Delivered to Wildlife Research Institute, Boise, Idaho. 1988.

National Park Service Management Policies. Prepared by U.S. Department of the Interior. 1988.

Parker, Steve. *Mammal; Eyewitness Books.* New York: Alfred A. Knopf. 1989.

Peregrine Fund Inc. Operation Report. Published at the World Center for Birds of Prey, Boise: 1990.

Petersen, David. *Racks: The Natural History of Antlers and the Animals That Wear Them.* Santa Barbara: Capra Press. 1991.

Russell, Osborne. *Journal of a Trapper;* edited by Aubrey L. Haines. Lincoln: University of Nebraska Press. 1953

Schmidt, John L., and Douglas L. Gilbert. *Big Game of North America.* Stackpole Books 1978.

Schullery, Paul. *The Bears of Yellowstone.* Yellowstone Library and Museum Association. 1980.

Schullery, Paul. Article for *Orion Nature Quarterly* titled "Drawing the Lines in Yellowstone: The American Bison as Symbol and Scourge." Autumn, 1986.

Schullery, Paul. Yellowstone technical writer, personal communications 1989 and 1990.

Singer, Francis, and Norman A. Bishop. Ungulate Grazing Effects on Yellowstone's Northern Winter Range– A Digest and part of a report to Congress. 1991.

Stelfox, Brad. Wildlife Info Cards prepared for Teton Science School. Jackson: Wildlife of the American West Art Museum.

Streubel, Donald. *Small Mammals of the Yellowstone Ecosystem.* Boulder; Roberts Rinehart. 1989.

Teton Science School (Kelly, Wyoming), "Looking at Elk," *Biologue Magazine,* Spring 1988.

Udvardy, Miklos D. F. *The Audubon Society Field Guide to North American Birds.* New York: Alfred A. Knopf. 1977.

Varley, John. Yellowstone's Chief of Research. Numerous personal communications between 1987 and 1991.

Whitaker Jr. John O., *The Audubon Society Field Guide to North American Mammals.* New York: Alfred A. Knopf. 1980.

Whitney, Stephen. *Western Forests.* New York: Alfred A. Knopf, Inc. Third Printing 1988.

Wilkinson, Todd. *Greater Yellowstone National Forests.* Helena: Falcon Press 1990.

Yellowstone Bison: Background and Issues. Publication by the State of Montana, National Park Service and U.S. Forest Service. May 1990.

Yellowstone Official Guide and Map. National Park Service. Reprinted 1989.